MYTH ALLEGORY AND GOSPEL

MYTH
ALLEGORY
AND
GOSPEL

An Interpretation of
J.R.R.Tolkien / C.S.Lewis
G.K.Chesterton / Charles Williams

By Edmund Fuller, Clyde S. Kilby, Russell Kirk,
John W. Montgomery & Chad Walsh

Edited by
John Warwick Montgomery
with Introduction, Revue Critique,
and Unpublished Letter from C. S. Lewis to the Editor

BETHANY FELLOWSHIP, INC.
Minneapolis, Minnesota

Library of Congress Cataloging in Publication Data

Montgomery, John Warwick.
Myth, Allegory, and Gospel.
1. Apologetics—20th century.
2. Chesterton, Gilbert Keith, 1874-1936.
3. Lewis, Clive Staples, 1898-1963.
4. Tolkien, John Ronald Reuel, 1892-1973
5. Williams, Charles, 1886-1945.
I. Fuller, Edmund, 1914-
II. Title.
BT1102.M66
239
74-1358
ISBN 0-87123-357-6
ISBN 0-87123-358-4 (pbk.)

Published by Bethany Fellowship, Inc.
6820 Auto Club Road, Minneapolis, Minnesota 55438

Printed in the United States of America

For

MY PARENTS

whose Montgomerian connections should
give them special insights into
leprechauns and hobbits

CONTENTS

PREFACE

ECUMENICITY IS LIKE HEAVEN: ALL DEM DAT'S
TALKING 'BOUT IT AIN'T A GITTIN' DERE. But the
lecture series which gave birth to the present volume is
not subject to this criticism. During the academic year
1969-1970, the Departments of Theology and English at DePaul
University and the Division of Philosophy and Religion of
the DePaul College threw hyper-specialization to the winds
and engaged in a commendable act of academic ecumenicity:
they co-sponsored a lecture series relating contemporary
literature to historic Christian faith. The University is Catholic,
and as moderator of the series they chose the undersigned,
a Protestant visiting professor. The subjects of the lectures
were Christian writers of both Catholic and Protestant
persuasion, and the lecturers likewise—with perhaps an
inevitable leaning toward those historical bridge-builders,
the Anglicans. The common element that bound the presentations together was the conviction that, in a day when many
are calling for a "demythologizing" of Christianity, more
attention should be paid to creative **littérateurs** who have
offered a more healthy alternative: the use of literary myth
to clarify and reinforce the creedal heart of the Christian
message.

Five presentations comprised the original series: Russell Kirk spoke on October 22, 1969; Edmund Fuller on November 19; Chad Walsh on December 3; Clyde S. Kilby on January 21, 1970; and on February 25, Mr. Robert Short gave an illustrated lecture on the theology of Charles Schulz's "Peanuts." The first four lectures appear in this volume with only slight revisions. Mr. Short's presentation, though delivered to an enthusiastic audience, had certain limitations which prohibited its inclusion in the published book. The editor had the privilege of chairing the first three sessions; two of his colleagues at the Trinity Seminary, Drs. David Wells and Clark Pinnock, kindly stood in for him at the last two sessions, when he was unavoidably called away from the Chicago area to serve as Honorary Fellow of Revelle College, University of California at San Diego. The editor's Introduction has been freshly prepared for this book; his essay, "The Chronicles of Narnia and the Adolescent Reader," first appeared in the September-October, 1959, issue of the journal **Religious Education**, and is here reprinted by permission, with slight updating; his French review of Professor Kilby's **Christian World of C. S. Lewis** is reproduced by agreement with the editorial board of the **Revue d'Histoire et de Philosophie Religieuses**, where it was published originally.

And now—in the words of the well-known poster—"Come to Middle Earth!"

JOHN WARWICK MONTGOMERY

22 April 1973
Easter Day: The Festival
   of the Great Eucatastrophe

1

John Warwick Montgomery

INTRODUCTION: The Apologists of Eucatastrophe

THE LORD OF THE RINGS ends, as a fairy-tale should, with what Tolkien calls a EUCATASTROPHE.

—W. H. Auden

The Birth of Christ is the eucatastrophe of Man's history. The Resurrection is the eucatastrophe of the story of the Incarnation. This story begins and ends in joy.

—J. R. R. Tolkien

Apologetics means of course Defence. The first question is — what do you propose to defend? Christianity, of course.

—C. S. Lewis

* * *

WHILE THE IDEA OF THE DEPAUL UNIVERSITY
LECTURE SERIES THAT HAS COME TO FRUITION IN
THIS VOLUME WAS STILL IN THE GERMINATION
STAGE, I corresponded with W. H. Auden about it.[1] He
suggested including George Macdonald — the 19th century
literary forefather of the writers we had chosen to treat—
as the subject of an essay in the series. Macdonald's inclusion
was not possible, but one of his characteristic remarks,
included by C. S. Lewis in his anthology of Macdonald,
can serve as the **point du départ** for understanding why
we selected Chesterton, Lewis, Tolkien, and Williams for
this series.

Aphorized Macdonald in **Love Thy Neighbour** (1st series):
"Our Lord never thought of being original." The four writers
treated in this volume have in common precisely this lack
of originality. To be sure, Macdonald's remark is paradoxi-
cal: No man in the world's history has ever had the impact
on other men's lives that the "unoriginal" Jesus had. How
could this have happened? we are forced to ask. Said Jesus
repeatedly: "I came down from heaven, not to do mine
own will, but the will of him that sent me" (John 6:38;
Luke 22:42; etc.). "Seek ye first the kingdom of God and
his righteousness," preached Jesus in the Sermon on the
Mount, "and all these [earthly] things shall be added unto
you" (Mt. 6:33). Our Lord's every word, act, and breath
were devoted to the faithful expression of the eternal will
of the Father, and thus it was, because "he who would
save his life shall lose it," Jesus' unoriginal selflessness
made Him the most original Person the world had or will
ever see: "wherefore God also hath highly exalted him,
and given him a name which is above every name: that

---

1. Auden's appreciation of Williams and Tolkien is of long standing, and derives both from
a poet's understanding of literary genius and from personal friendship. Cf. Monroe K. Spears,
The Poetry of W. H. Auden (New York: Oxford University Press, 1963). Auden wrote the original
review of **The Fellowship of the Ring** for **The New York Times**, and a perceptive article, "Good
and Evil in **The Lord of the Rings**" (from which our introductory quotation is taken) in the
Tolkien Journal, III/1 (1967), 5-8. To that same issue of the **Tolkien Journal**, celebrating Tolkien's
seventy-fifth birthday, Professor Kilby contributed an essay on "Tolkien As Scholar and Artist"
(pp. 9-11).

at the name of Jesus every knee should bow, of things in heaven, and things in earth, and things under the earth; and that every tongue should confess that Jesus Christ is Lord, to the glory of God the Father" (Phil. 2:9-11).

Chesterton, Lewis, Tolkien, and Williams display an analogous—and to the unbeliever, an inexplicable and infuriating—combination of ingenuousness and genius. On the one hand, no 20th century writers in the English-speaking world have had such an intensive and extensive impact on the intelligentsia in the sphere of ultimate commitment. Cambridge University's David Daiches, an agnostic professor of English under whom I studied at Cornell, considered Lewis the very symbol of religious revival in England after World War II. In 1972, the sixth year Ballantine Books published Tolkien in paperback in the U.S.A., two million copies of their editions of his works were sold—to say nothing of 175,000 Tolkien calendars!

And yet these writers seem almost to make a fetish of unoriginality: Williams employs as his fundamental and recurrent leitmotifs the themes of Substitution and the City ("Your Life and Death are with Your Neighbor" is the motto of the City) which are consciously derived from the central teachings of creedal Christianity, as he witnesses their development in **The Descent of the Dove: A History of the Holy Spirit in the Church.** Williams' powerful delineation of the demonic, especially conveyed in the supernatural novels, **All Hallows' Eve** and **Descent into Hell** —a comprehension of the strategy of evil which Auden, in his Introduction to **The Descent of the Dove**, considers one of Williams' greatest strengths—is a direct product of Holy Writ, as any reader of Williams' **Witchcraft** will recognize.[2]

2. See my **Shape of the Past** (Ann Arbor, Mich.: Edwards Brothers, 1963), pp. 24-25, 28, 150-51, and the references there cited. Cf. also Dorothy L. Sayers, "Charles Williams: A Poet's Critic," in her collection, **The Poetry of Search and the Poetry of Statement** (London: Gollancz, 1963), pp. 69-90; Raymond Chapman, **The Ruined Tower** (London: Bles, 1961), **passim**; and Rosalie V. Otters, "Charles Williams' Philosophy of History" (unpublished Master's thesis, Department of Church History and the History of Christian Thought, Trinity Evangelical Divinity School, 1971).

Tolkien, an English philologist by profession, so carefully limits his imagery to the archetypal symbols of Celtic and medieval deep myth and the verities of the Christian tradition that in the judgment of a recent critic he displays but "erratic originality," so that "his earnest vision seems syncretic, his structure a collage, and his feeling antiquarian." [3] How odd that college students should not have been turned off by so "antiquarian" a work as **The Lord of the Rings**; how peculiar that in a previous national election they wore buttons inscribed, "Vote for Gandalf,"and that they long beyond longing—in the words of the Tolkien Society poster—to "come to Middle Earth"!

A most vitriolic critic of Lewis refers to him throughout her book as "vulgar," "coarse," "stupid," "pinheaded," and—though their compatibility of that idea is somewhat in doubt—"soap-box" yet "suburban." Her rage particularly focuses on his "intellectual orthodoxy" and "fundamentalism." Says she of Lewis and Dorothy Sayers (who might equally have been included in the present series of lectures): "Both these writers could be described, not too metaphorically, as fundamentalists. They claim that all the answers which the human mind requires, to form an adequate picture of the universe it inhabits, are to be found in the Christian revelation." [4] Along the same line, process theology liberal Norman Pittenger castigated Lewis in the pages of **Christian Century** (October 1, 1958) for his theologically untrained naïveté in basing his faith on "mechanical" authority—on

---

3. Catherine R. Stimpson, **J. R. R. Tolkien** ("Columbia Essays on Modern Writers," 41; New York: Columbia University Press, 1969), p. 9. For more helpful treatments, see Paul H. Kocher, **Master of Middle-earth: The Fiction of J. R. R. Tolkien** (Boston: Houghton Mifflin, 1972), and Lin Carter, **Tolkien: A Look behind "The Lord of the Rings"** (New York: Ballantine Books, 1969); cf. also Gracia Fay Ellwood, **Good News from Tolkien's Middle Earth** (Grand Rapids, Mich.: Eerdmans, 1970).

4. Kathleen Nott, **The Emperor's Clothes** (Bloomington: Indiana University Press, 1958), p. 48 (for her other references to Lewis mentioned above, see pp. 8, 43, 68, 76, 105-06, 176, 254ff.). A devastating, and well deserved, review of the original British printing of Miss Nott's book was written by John W. Simons for **Commonweal**, April 22, 1955; said he: "Her book is strewn with the sophistries she would foist upon others." Chad Walsh, in his **C. S. Lewis: Apostle to the Skeptics**, has correctly distinguished Lewis' "classical Christianity" from sociologically rightist, American "Bible-belt" fundamentalism.

what has "grown up in the church and won the assent of great doctors." Lewis, who seldom replied to public criticism, preferring a more self-effacing role, did answer Dr. Pittenger (**Christian Century**, November 26, 1958), and the conlusion of the riposte is too pertinent to our discussion not to be quoted:

When I began, Christianity came before the great mass of my unbelieving fellow-countrymen either in the highly emotional form offered by revivalists or in the unintelligible language of highly cultured clergymen. Most men were reached by neither. My task was therefore simply that of a **translator**—one turning Christian doctrine, or what he believed to be such, into the vernacular, into language that unscholarly people would attend to and could understand. For this purpose a style more guarded, more **nuancé**, finelier shaded, more rich in fruitful ambiguities—in fact, a style more like Dr. Pittenger's own—would have been worse than useless. It would not only have failed to enlighten the common reader's understanding; it would have aroused his suspicion. He would have thought, poor soul, that I was facing both ways, sitting on the fence, offering at one moment what I withdrew the next, and generally trying to trick him. I may have made theological errors. My manner may have been defective. Others may do better hereafter. I am ready, if I am young enough, to learn. Dr. Pittenger would be a more helpful critic if he advised a cure as well as asserting many diseases. How does he himself do such work? What methods, and with what success, does he employ when he is trying to convert the great mass of storekeepers, lawyers, realtors, morticians, policemen and artisans who surround him in his own city?

One thing at least is sure. If the real theologians had tackled this laborious work of translation about a hundred years ago, when they began to lose touch with the people (for whom Christ died), there would have been no place for me.

Chesterton, in the first paragraph of his continually reprinted classic **Orthodoxy**, testified of the content of his book: "I will not call it my philosophy; for I did not make it. God and humanity made it; and it made me." In essence, Chesterton and the "Anglo-Oxford Christians" are men of genius precisely because of their unoriginality. Like the centurion of whom Jesus said, "I have not found so great faith, no, not in Israel," they are "men set under authority" (Luke 7:8-9). They have nothing which they would term "**their** philosophy." What they write of, they did not make. It made them. And what, precisely, is the "it"? In C. S. Lewis' words, quoted at the outset: "Christianity, of course." Let us hear **in extenso** again from Lewis, since his analysis of what it means to affirm and defend Christianity is precisely the viewpoint shared by all four of our writers:

> We are to defend Christianity itself—the faith preached by the Apostles, attested by the Martyrs, embodied in the Creeds, expounded by the Fathers. This must be clearly distinguished from the whole of what any one of us may think about God and Man. Each of us has his individual emphasis: each holds, in addition to the Faith, many opinions which seem to him to be consistent with it and true and important. And so perhaps they are. But as apologists it is not our business to defend **them**. We are defending Christianity; not "my religion." . . . A clearly maintained distinction between what the Faith actually says and what you would like it to have said or what you understand or what you personally find helpful or think probable, forces your audience to realize that you are tied to your data just as the scientist is tied by the results of the experiments; that you are not just saying what you like. This immediately helps them to realize that what is being discussed is a question about objective fact— not gas about ideals and points of view. . . .

> The new truth which you do not know and which you need must, in the very nature of things, be hidden precisely in the doctrines you least like and least understand. It is just the same here as in science. The phenomenon which is troublesome, which doesn't fit in with the current scientific theories, is the phenomenon which compels reconsideration and thus leads to new knowledge. Science progresses because scientists, instead of running away from such troublesome phenomena or hushing them up, are constantly seeking them out. In the same way, there will be progress in Christian knowledge only as long as we accept the challenge of the difficult or repellent doctrines. A "liberal" Christianity which considers itself free to alter the Faith whenever the Faith

looks perplexing or repellent **must** be completely stagnant. Progress is made only into a **resisting** material.[5]

* * *

But just as there are numerous ways to skin a cat, so there are numerous ways to defend Christianity. Lewis has just noted and rightly rejected the "liberal" method: change the substance of the Faith to make it more palatable or "relevant" to the secular situation. Such an approach turns the medicine of immortality into the germ of the disease and leaves the patient to die of the deception. But even in the realm of what Chesterton described as orthodoxy, apologetics is a plural and not a singular. The late Edward John Carnell once remarked that there are as many apologetics as there are facts in the world.

In an article of mine on a Moslem apologist published some years ago, I classified orthodox apologetic techniques in three categories: Rational defenses (apriorism, presuppositionalism, internal self-consistency), Objective Empirical defenses (miracle, fulfilled prophecy, conformity with the historical and scientific facts of experience), and Subjective Empirical defenses (the religious position is personally meaningful and self-validating in the life of the believer).[6] Rational defenses have the least biblical precedent, and the classic expression of this approach, the Ontological Proof for God's existence, has never claimed the allegiance of more than a few Christian apologists. The insuperable problem with apriorism is its begging of the question: why should the non-Christian begin where the Christian begins?[7]

Thus most apologetic endeavors through Christian history

---

5. C. S. Lewis, "Christian Apologetics," in his **God in the Dock: Essays on Theology and Ethics**, ed. Walter Hooper (Grand Rapids, Mich.: Eerdmans, 1970), pp. 90-91.

6. "The Apologetic Approach of Muhammed Ali and Its Implications for Christian Apologetics," **Muslim World**, LI/2 (April, 1961), 111-22 (cf. author's corrigendum in the July, 1961, **Muslim World**).

7. Cf. my critiques of Gordon Clark and Cornelius Van Til, in the Festschriften for these two Christian presuppositionalists: **The Philosophy of Gordon Clark**, ed. Ronald Nash (Nutley, N. J.: Presbyterian and Reformed Publishing Co., 1968) and **Jerusalem and Athens**, ed. Geehan (**ibid.**, 1971).

have been Empirical: following the biblical model, Christian believers have tried to show how the evidences of miracle, prophecy, and inner experience compel consideration of the Christian starting-point as the most adequate approach for understanding man and the world. Predominance has been given to objective evidence, and for good reason. The scriptural apologetic makes miracle and prophecy central, and the Apologists of Patristic times, who closely followed the Apostolic footsteps, went and did likewise. Today's Analytical movement in philosophy has redirected attention to fundamental epistemological considerations, and has rightly insisted that if a religion wishes to make meaningful claims to factual truth, it must offer meaningfully objective evidence in support of those claims. Objective, historical evidence for Christian truth has the great merit of openness to public inquiry; it cannot easily be ignored as the product of inner wish-fulfillment. Objective facts are difficult to dispense with **ad hominem**—by the subtle or not-so-subtle redirection of the argument from the issue of the truth of the Faith to the psychology, needs, and personal hang-ups of the apologist.

Hesitancy in offering Subjective defenses for the Gospel has been increased by the history of such argumentation in the last two centuries. Kant so intimidated traditional, Objective apologists that a Subjective reaction set in through the work of Schleiermacher and Ritschl, leading directly to the "liberal" dilutions of Christian faith so perceptively criticized by Lewis. In the half century after Kant's death, a no less momentous reaction occurred when Kierkegaard opposed Hegelian idealism with the battle cry, "Truth is subjectivity." From Kierkegaard's (genuinely Christian) subjectivity developed the atheistic subjectivity of 20th century existentialism on the one hand (Heidegger, Sartre), and the reductionistic, demythologizing existentialism of most contemporary German theology (Bultmann—whose position developed from Heidegger's—and the post-Bultmannian "New Hermeneutic"). The demythologizers have peeled away at the onion of objective Christian truth, claiming that if one can just get rid of the layers of miraculous symbolism created by a prescientific age, the "self-authenticating," existential heart of the Christian faith will be revealed in its purity to modern man. But secular man observes the process with little more than amusement, since as the "layers" of Incarnation, Virgin Birth, and Resurrection are discarded, nothing whatever of the Christian basics seems to be left, and the secularist has every reason to wonder if "existential self-authentication" is not the product of theological self-hypnosis—wish-fulfillment writ large, in which one thinks he can have the cake of Christian hope while at the same time masticating it with the teeth of rationalistic biblical criticism.

Neither has fundamentalist inwardness encouraged apologists in the direction of a Subjective apologetic. The fundamentalist, appalled by modernistic corruptions of the Gospel in pseudo-intellectual dress, quickly learned to attribute all such efforts to "the wisdom of this world." In contrast to such intellectualizing, the fundamentalist came to rely on his conversion experience and the evidence of salvation in his personal experience. "Testimonies" to "meeting Christ" (remarkably similar, at least in their subjectivity, with existential "encounters"!) and inward answers to prayer became the substitute for Objective evidence in presenting the Christian faith to others. But the very personal, individualistic nature of this evidence has left it vulnerable to the criticism equally applicable to existentialism: how does one know that the experience so described represents reality, and is not simply a product of the believer's own psychological processes? Accounts of parallel evangelical conversion experiences (Begbie's **Twice-born Men**, etc.), though helpful, do not really meet this objection, since one can also collect conversion experiences relative to other world-faiths (e.g., many of the cases in William James' **Varieties of Religious Experience**), and the mutually contradictory nature of these various religions eliminates the possibility that they can all be true.

And yet the need for a responsible Subjective apologetic for Christian truth remains. The ongoing, self-perpetuating juggernaut of scientific technology has alienated many in our society from the ideals of scientific objectivity. Objectivity seems for them (irrationally, but, after all, they are trying to run from rationality!) the source of pollution, depersonalization, and a culture that will spend billions on a moon shot and quibble about appropriations to clean up the ghetto. Young people in particular drop out and freak out as a protest against such hyper-objectifying of life and its values. They seek another kind of answer—an answer perhaps hidden in the Subjective depths of their own souls. But what key will unlock this hidden treasure? Some go the whole experiential route: sex, drugs, masochism, satanic occultism. Others seek salvation in the inward-focused Eastern religions.[8] But the path of drugs and the occult is strewn with the wrecked lives of those who have given themselves to these false gods.[9] And, as Arthur Koestler has so definitively shown in the account of his frustrating pilgrimage in search of Eastern wisdom, the ambiguities of the Tantristic religions open them to the most immoral, destructive, and demonic possibilities.[10]

Might literary creativity offer a way through this labyrinth? Can literature perhaps succeed where these deceptive paths have failed?

A drainless shower
Of light is poesy: 'tis the supreme of power

declared Keats in **Sleep and Poetry**. As a dream while asleep can touch the depths of our being, could not the literature of wakefulness shower with light and supreme power the landscape of religious concern, and provide the

---

8. Cf. John H. Garabedian and Orde Coombs, **Eastern Religions in the Electric Age** (New York: Grosset & Dunlap, 1969).

9. Montgomery, **Principalities and Powers: The World of the Occult** (Minneapolis: Bethany Fellowship, 1973), especially pp. 121-50 ("The Land of Mordor") and 188-90 ("The Gospel according to LSD").

10. Arthur Koestler, **The Lotus and the Robot** (New York: Macmillan, 1961), especially pp. 236-41, 268-75.

Subjective attestation of Christian truth for which men long? The writers with whom we are dealing regard literature as such a means of grace, but their viewpoint is immensely more sophisticated than that of 19th century Romanticism— or of 20th century Realism.

* * *

The universal or near-universal appeal of great literature to Christian and non-Christian alike holds out the possibility of a more solid Subjective bridge by which unbelievers might pass into the Kingdom. If the Faith can be found mirrored in the great literary productions of the time, would this not lead the secular reader to a new appreciation of that "Faith once delivered to the saints"?[11]

The most common way in which this case is argued today by Christian interpreters of literature could be termed (with apologies to mystical theology) the **via negativa**, or negative path. Here an effort is made to show that secular literary classics (1) depict the sinful, fallen human condition in exact accord with biblical anthropology, and (2) demonstrate that all contemporary secular ways of salvation are deceptive and unable to solve man's dilemma. By process of elimination, then, the reader is brought to a consideration of the Christian answer as the only, or at very least the most meaningful, solution to his fallen condition. Some examples will make this approach clear. Albert Camus' **La Peste** (The Plague) accurately describes the human condition as mortally diseased and no more capable of being cured from within than is the city of Oran able to be freed from its pestilential agonies by medical efforts within it. George Orwell's **1984** shows the logical consequences of man's "nasty" and "brutish" life (to use the terms of 17th

---

11. Cf. Amos N. Wilder, **Theology and Modern Literature** (Cambridge, Mass.: Harvard University Press, 1958); William R. Mueller, **The Prophetic Voice in Modern Fiction** (New York: Association Press, 1959); Nathan A. Scott, Jr., **The Broken Center: Studies in the Theological Horizon of Modern Literature** (New Haven: Yale University Press, 1966); Nathan A. Scott, Jr. (ed.), **Adversity and Grace: Studies in Recent American Literature** ("Essays in Divinity," IV; Chicago: University of Chicago Press, 1968); Kurt F. Reinhardt, **The Theological Novel of Modern Europe** (New York: Frederick Ungar, 1969).

century atheist Hobbes, whose **Leviathan** is in many ways a forerunner of **1984**): will-to-power leads, by way of the totalitarianism of our day (National Socialism, Marxism), to complete thought control and absolute dehumanization. Franz Kafka's **Der Prozess** (The Trial) is the account of a man (Joseph K—the author Kafka—and, through him, Everyman) who is brought to ultimate judgment, though on no specific charge; and he recognizes (testifying, we would say, to the fact of original sin) that he deserves this, and so does humanity in general.

False solutions to this human dilemma of sin and deserved judgment are revealed for what they are in such contemporary works as William Golding's **Lord of the Flies**, John Updike's **Rabbit, Run** (and recent sequel, **Rabbit Redux**), and Samuel Beckett's **En attendant Godot** (Waiting for Godot). Golding's account of the savagery of well brought-up English schoolboys marooned on an island destroys the illusion that good education, civilization, and culture can eradicate man's bestiality. Updike reveals the hollowness of the American dream of the adolescent high-school hero who can attain salvation through conformity to the American Way of Life. Beckett systematically destroys all the pretences of redemption-by-works in modern life—aesthetics, altruism, intellectualism, achievement—and sees secular existence as a "blathering in the void":

VLADIMAR: And where were we yesterday evening according to you?

ESTRAGON: How would I know? In another compartment. There's no lack of void.

VLADIMIR: (**sure of himself**), Good. We weren't here yesterday evening. Now what did we do yesterday evening?

ESTRAGON: Do?

VLADIMIR: Try and remember.

ESTRAGON: Do . . . I suppose we blathered.

VLADIMIR: (**controlling himself**). About what?

ESTRAGON: Oh . . . this and that I suppose, nothing in particular. (**With assurance**.) Yes, now I remember, yesterday evening we spent blathering
about nothing in particular. That's been going
on now for half a century.

In applying these literary evidences of man's sinfulness,
deserved judgment, and incapacity to save himself, the
Christian interpreter-apologist operates on the basis of the
Augustinian principle enunciated at the beginning of **The
Confessions**: "Fecisti nos ad te et inquietum est cor nostrum,
donec requiescat in te" (Thou hast made us for Thyself
and our heart is restless until it rest in Thee). This is
the principle of the "God-shaped blank": each heart is
like a picture-puzzle with one piece missing, and the missing
piece, which alone will give meaning to all the rest, is
in the shape of a Cross. Contemporary literature can outline
negatively the shape of the missing piece. Thus the non-
Christian can be brought to see that only the Gospel is
capable of fulfilling his deepest needs.

But the sinner seeks to fit other answers into the empty
space in his heart; he imagines the possibility of solutions
for the human dilemma so realistically described in modern
secular literature. As a deterent to this tendency, is it not
possible to go beyond the **via negativa** and affirmatively
trace the positive message of Christian redemption by way
of literary motifs? Here more ambitious literary apologists
appeal to the concept of the "Christ image": the veiled
figure of Christ which appears in a multitude of guises
in secular literary classics. Consider the list of possibilities
to which chapters are devoted in Moseley's **Pseudonyms
of Christ in the Modern Novel**:

Christ as Tragic Hero: Conrad's **Lord Jim**
Christ as Death-in-Life and Life-in-Death: Dostoyevsky's
   Crime and Punishment
Christ as the Archetypal Son: Turgenev's **Fathers and Sons**
Christ as Artist and Lover: D. H. Lawrence's **Sons and Lovers**
Christ as Doomed Youth: Remarque's **All Quiet on the
   Western Front**

Christ as the Missing Orient: Fitzgerald's **The Great Gatsby**
Christ as Social Scapegoat: Faulkner's **Light in August**
Christ as One Avatar: Forster's **Passage to India**
Christ as the Brother of Man: Steinbeck's **Grapes of Wrath**
Christ as Marxist Variant:
    Silone's **Bread and Wine**,
    Malraux' **Man's Fate**, and
    Koestler's **Darkness at Noon**
Christ as Existentialist Antichrist: Camus' **The Stranger**
Christ as the Old Champion: Hemingway's **The Old Man
    and the Sea**[12]

This series of Christic interpretations begins bravely
enough: few would have difficulty in recognizing a Christ-
figure in Conrad's Lord Jim, or in the work of Dostoyevsky—
and one wonders why Melville's Billy Budd did not strike
the interpreter as an even more obvious example. But
D. H. Lawrence's **Sons and Lovers**? Christ as "Marxist Variant" and even "Existentialist Antichrist"? One is reminded
of Bruce Barton's characterizations of Jesus (**The Man No-
body Knows**) during the heyday of Protestant modernism:
Jesus "the Executive," "the Outdoor Man," "the Sociable
Man"—and, to be sure, "the Founder of Modern Business"
("Wist ye not that I must be about my Father's business?").
One thinks also of the "Christ" of the death-of-God movement, who was so kenotically hidden in the process of history
and the social movements of the day that in no particular
respect at all could he be identified necessarily with the
Jesus of the New Testament. If virtually anything is a
Christ-figure, nothing is a Christ-figure, and the apologist
has fallen back entirely into the miasma of an uncritical,
individualistic subjectivism. This is brought out hilariously
by Frederick C. Crews as he "discovers" a Christ-image
in A. A. Milne's **Winnie-the-Pooh**; here is the crux (!) passage
of his essay, "**O Felix Culpa!** The Sacramental Meaning
of **Winnie-the-Pooh**":

---

12. Edwin M. Moseley, **Pseudonymns of Christ in the Modern Novel** (Pittsburgh: University
of Pittsburgh Press, 1962). See also: F. W. Dillistone, **The Novelist and the Passion Story** (New
York: Sheed & Ward, 1960); Donald L. Deffner, "Christ-figure in Contemporary Literature,"
Concordia Theological Monthly, XXXIV (May, 1963), 278-83; Robert Detweiler, "Christ and the
Christ Figure in American Fiction," **Christian Scholar**, XLVII/2 (Summer, 1964), 111-24.

Searching for a literary Savior is, if I may confide in the reader, often a rather trying affair, since this personage must be an epitome of meekness and at the same time act as a strong moral guide for the other characters. In **Pooh** we have no dearth of meek characters, but a frustrating want of moral pronouncements. Yet there is one Character, blessedly, Who outdoes all the others in humility while managing, at one dramatic moment, to reveal His true identity in a divine Uttering: "A little Consideration," He says, "a little Thought for Others, makes all the difference." What an electrifying effect this produces on the reader! At one stroke we have been transported back across all the materialistic heresies of the modern world, back safely across the wicked Counter-Reformation into the purity of Cranmer, Henry the Eighth, the early Church, and the Sermon on the Mount. Here we have none of the hypocrisy of the crafty Loyola, none of the foaming frenzy of the Anabaptists, but a simple assertion of the Golden Rule. The Speaker is of course Eeyore, the Lowly One, the Despised, Acquainted with Grief. His dictum of pure **caritas** is the moral standard by which every action of the lesser characters in **Winnie-the-Pooh-** must be severely judged.[13]

Is there no way to avoid such bizarre results in the quest for a positive literary apologetic? The development of firm, biblically grounded criteria for the Christ-figure would offer the best protection—but there is a built-in difficulty: no literary character can in fact **be** the historic Christ, so the character's inadequacies and sins will automatically create tension with the biblical picture of the Savior, and to that extent reduce the effectiveness of the literary portrayal as an apologetic. Can a different orientation put us on firmer ground?

Suppose that the fallen race had kept a primordial realization of its separation from God through sinful self-centeredness and of its specific need for redemption through the divine-human conquest of the evil powers arrayed against

---

13. Frederick C. Crews, **The Pooh Perplex** (New York: Dutton Paperbacks, 1965), p. 58. In this magnificent **tour de force** "it is discovered that the true meaning of the Pooh stories is not as simple as is usually believed, but for proper elucidation requires the combined efforts of several academicians of varying critical persuasions."

it. Suppose within each human heart this realization were etched beyond effacement. The sinner would of course repress this knowledge, for his sin would be too painful to bear and his egotism would not want to face redemption apart from his own works-righteousness. Though "the invisible things of God are clearly seen," so that men are "without excuse," they become "vain in their imaginations" and their "foolish hearts are darkened" (Rom. 1:20-21). This darkening of the heart would quite naturally take the form of a repression of the natural knowledge of God's redemptive plan to the subconscious level, where it could be ignored consciously; but its eradication from the psyche could never occur. Under these circumstances, redemptive knowledge would surface not in a direct fashion but by way of symbolic patterns—visible not only to the sensitive psychoanalyst, but also to the folklorist whose material "bubbles up" collectively from the subconscious of the race. Literature in this special sense could therefore reflect the Christian story in an objective sense and trigger conscious acceptance of it. Is this perhaps the background of Paul's literary appeal on the Areopagus: "As certain also of your own poets have said, For we are also his offspring" (Acts 17:28)?

Jungian analytical psychotherapy has indeed identified such redemptive "archetypes," or fundamental and universal symbolic patterns, which appear equally in the physical liturgies of ancient alchemists and in the dreams of contemporary business men. Religious phenomenologists— the greatest being Mircea Eliade—have discovered these motifs in the most widely diversified primitive and sophisti- cated religions. Concludes Eliade after examining one of the most basic archetypal themes: "At the 'beginning' as well as at the 'end' of the religious history of Man, we find the same 'yearning for Paradise.' If we take into account the fact that the 'yearning for Paradise' is equally discern- ible in the general religious attitude of early man we have the right to assume that the mystical memory of a blessedness without history haunts man from the moment he becomes aware of his situation in the cosmos."[14] Thus does the great universal literary tradition of Utopia point back, with inexpressible longings, to the Garden. And thus consciously-produced modern literary endeavors can appeal to a yearning in every human heart. One thinks of James Hilton's **Lost Horizon**—or the captivating Lerner-Loewe musical, **Brigadoon**. In that Edenic town, the people are redemptively protected from witches when they sleep by a vicarious act of their pastor; as they sleep, one hundred years wondrously pass.

Tommy: But at night when you go to sleep; what's it like?

Mr. Lundie: Well, for me, 'tis like being carried on shadowy arms to some far-off cloud an' there I float till mornin'. An' yet, sometimes I think I hear strange voices.

Tommy: Voices?

Mr. Lundie: Aye. They say no words I can remember. But they're voices filled with a fearful longin'; an' often they seem to be callin' me back. I've pondered it when I'm awake; an' I think—I have a feelin' I'm hearin' the outside world. There mus' be lots of folk out there who'd like a Brigadoon.[15]

Mythology and folktale are especially pregnant with archetypal significance. In an important study on "Recurrent Themes in Myths and Mythmaking," Kluckhohn provides rigorous attestation of anthropologist Lévi-Strauss' contention that there is an "astounding similarity between myths collected in widely different regions" of the world.[16] Kluckhohn and Moench used Murdock's "world ethnographic

14. Mircea Eliade, "The Yearning for Paradise in Primitive Tradition," in **Myth and Mythmaking**, ed. Henry A. Murray (New York: George Braziller, 1960), p. 73.

15. Alan Jay Lerner, **Brigadoon** (New York: Coward-McCann, 1947), pp. 88-89. This musical first opened in the Ziegfeld Theatre in New York City in March, 1947—soon after the end of World War II, when America's utopian longings were revivified.

16. Claude Lévi-Strauss, "The Structural Study of Myth," **Journal of American Folklore**, LXVIII (1955), 428-45; cf. the same author's "Structure et dialectique" in the Festschrift for Roman Jakobson, edited by Morris Halle (The Hague: Mouton, 1957), pp. 289-94.

sample"[17] to analyze recurrent mythical themes in fifty cultures, "distributed about evenly among Murdock's six major regions (Circum-Mediterranean, Negro Africa, East Eurasia, Insular Pacific, North America, South America)." Two of the most prominent recurrent themes are the Flood ("a universal or near-universal theme in mythology" which "hardly seems plausible to attribute to Jewish-Christian sources"),[18] and the "Slaying of Monsters": "This theme appears in thirty-seven of our fifty cultures, and here the distribution approaches equality save for a slightly greater frequency in North America and the Insular Pacific. . . . In Bantu Africa (and beyond) a hero is born to a woman who survives after a monster has eaten her spouse (and everyone else). The son immediately turns into a man, slays a monster or monsters, restores his people."[19]

Does not this "slaying of a monster" have a familiar ring to it (our pun on Tolkien's One Ring is not unintentional!)? Gustaf Aulén has demonstrated the centrality of the Christus Victor motif to the entire New Testament message: Jesus, born of a woman, is in fact the Divine Christ who conquers the Evil Power that has brought the race into bondage, and thereby restores mankind.[20] From such universal—and therefore impressively Objective—archetypal Motifs can the Christian littérateur draw his themes and patterns, thereby creating stories that, if sensitively and artistically executed, are sure to strike to the deep reaches of man's being and point him toward the Christ who fulfilled the myths and legends of the world.

It is this literary apologetic for the Gospel—the Great Eucatastrophe—that unites the writers discussed in the

---

17. G. P. Murdock, "World Ethnographic Sample," **American Anthropologist**, LIX (1957), 664-88.
18. Cf. Montgomery, **The Quest for Noah's Ark** (Minneapolis: Bethany Fellowship, 1972), **passim.**
19. Clyde Kluckhohn "Recurrent Themes in Myths and Mythmaking," in **Myth and Mythmaking** (**op. cit.**), p. 51.
20. Gustaf Aulén, **Christus Victor**, trans. A. G. Hebert (New York: Macmillan, 1956); cf. my "Short Critique of Gustaf Aulén's **Christus Victor**," printed as an appendix in my **Chytraeus on Sacrifice** (St. Louis, Mo.: Concordia, 1962).

present volume. To be sure, others have performed this role in other ages; one thinks particularly of Edmund Spenser[21] and Johann Valentin Andreae[22] before the cataclysmic "great divide" that separates "Old Western man" and the Classical-Christian epoch from the modern secular era. But few have performed this labor of genius as well as our writers in the desolate landscape of post-Christian paganism. We do not claim that the writers here treated all lower their buckets to the same depth into "the Well at the World's End": there is an immense distance between **The Lord of the Rings** and Chesterton's **Flying Inn**. We can, in fact, offer the following schematic typology:

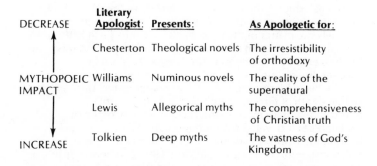

DECREASE ↑	Literary Apologist:	Presents:	As Apologetic for:
	Chesterton	Theological novels	The irresistibility of orthodoxy
MYTHOPOEIC IMPACT	Williams	Numinous novels	The reality of the supernatural
	Lewis	Allegorical myths	The comprehensiveness of Christian truth
INCREASE ↓	Tolkien	Deep myths	The vastness of God's Kingdom

But granting the legitimacy of this analysis (vindication of which is left to the judgment of readers as addicted to this literary genre as the editor), it would be hard to deny the common thrust of all four writers: in a century when most secularists and theologians are busily stripping away alleged "myths" (in their sense of "non-factual stories") from Christianity, our apologists of eucatastrophe

---

21. See, in addition to Lewis' **Allegory of Love** and **English Literature in the 16th Century**, Virgil K. Whitaker, **The Religious Basis of Spenser's Thought** ("Stanford University Series: Language and Literature," VII/3; New York: Gordian Press, 1966); A. C. Hamilton, **The Structure of Allegory in "The Faerie Queene"** (Oxford: Clarendon Press, 1964); M. Pauline Parker, **The Allegory of the "Faerie Queene"** (Oxford: Clarendon Press, 1962).

22. See Montgomery, **Cross and Crucible: Johann Valentin Andreae (1586-1654), Phoenix of the Theologians** ("International Archives of the History of Ideas," 55; The Hague: Martinus Nijhoff, 1973), 2 vols.

find in myth (in the proper sense of archetypal tale) the objectifying literary apologetic for Christian truth—a pointer nonpareil to the fulfillment of mankind's longings in the factuality of the Gospel Story.

Let us, in conclusion, hear Lewis' confessions of mythopoeic faith—the first, from his spiritual autobiography, **Surprised by Joy**, in a passage perceptively anthologized by Edmund Fuller; the second from his seminal essay, "Myth Became Fact":

> I was by now too experienced in literary criticism to regard the Gospels as myths. They had not the mythical taste. And yet the very matter which they set down in their artless, historical fashion—those narrow, unattractive Jews, too blind to the mythical wealth of the Pagan world around them—was precisely the matter of the great myths. If ever a myth had become fact, had been incarnated, it would be just like this. Myths were like it in one way. Histories were like it in another. But nothing was simply like it. And no person was like the Person it depicted; as real, as recognizable, through all that depth of time, as Plato's Socrates or Boswell's Johnson (ten times more so than Eckermann's Goethe or Lockhart's Scott), yet also numinous, lit by a light from beyond the world, a god. But if a god—we are no longer polytheists—then not a god, but God. Here and here only in all time the myth must become fact; the Word, flesh; God, Man. This is not "a religion," nor "a philosophy." It is the summing up and actuality of them all.[23]

> We must not be ashamed of the mythical radiance resting on our theology. We must not be nervous about "parallels" and "Pagan Christs": they **ought** to be there—it would be a stumbling block if they weren't. We must not, in false spirituality, withhold our imaginative welcome. If God chooses to be mythopoeic—and is not the sky itself a myth—shall we refuse to be **mythopathic**? For this is the marriage of heaven and earth: Perfect Myth and Perfect Fact: claiming not only our love and our obedience, but also our wonder and delight,

---

23. Edmund Fuller (ed.), **Affirmations of God and Man** (New York: Association Press, 1967), p. 37.

addressed to the savage, the child, and the poet in each one of us no less than to the moralist, the scholar, and the philosopher.[24]

24. C. S. Lewis, "Myth Became Fact," in his **God in the Dock** (**op. cit.**), p. 67. Cf. the chapter on Myth in Lewis' **An Experiment in Criticism** (Cambridge, Eng.: Cambridge University Press, 1961), pp. 40-49.

2

Russell Kirk

chesteRTON, MAOMEN, ANO MAOHOUSES

NO MAN OF HIS TIME DEFENDED MORE PASSIONATELY THE CAUSE OF SANITY AND "CENTRICITY" THAN DID G. K. CHESTERTON, despite his aversion to watches and his uncalculated picturesqueness of dress. But no imaginative writer touched more often than did Chesterton upon lunacy, real or alleged: a prospect of his age with the madhouse for its background.

"It is, indeed, an absurd exaggeration to say that we are all mad," Chesterton writes in **Lunacy and Letters**, "just as it is true that we are none of us perfectly healthy. If there were to appear in the world a perfectly sane man, he would certainly be locked up. The terrible simplicity

with which he would walk over our minor morbidities, our
sulky vanities and malicious self-righteousness; the
elephantine innocence with which he would ignore our fictions of civilization—these would make him a thing more
desolating and inscrutable than a thunderbolt or a beast
of prey. It may be that the great prophets who appeared
to mankind as mad were in reality raving with an impotent
sanity."

What Burke called "metaphysical madness," the delu-
sions of the ideologue and the neoterist, was the modern
affliction against which Chesterton contended. The Library
of the British Museum, Chesterton remarks, "discharges
a great many of the functions of a private madhouse."
Against the sort of lunacy encountered in libraries, and
the sort encountered in public affairs, Chesterton took his
stand. Madhouses, public or private, loom large in seven
of his fantastic romances; madmen pop up in high places.
In our era, his argument runs, some of the wisest and
best men may find themselves in Bedlam: for the madman
and the rogue manipulating madmen are in power.

Since Chesterton wrote, madhouses have multiplied; but
seldom do they display the outward amenities of that asylum
(designed by Lucifer) in which the zealot and the atheist
of **The Ball and the Cross** end their flight from the police.
Once, pursuing Scottish historical researches, I strolled by
accident into a private madhouse to be proud of: a sixteenth-
century mansion, once a manse, all flowers and lawns within
its high stone dykes. The typical "mental institution" of
our twentieth century, however, is more hygienic, more
scientific, more grim, and more voracious: no one could
mistake it for a parsonage.

As we slide away from the normality that Chesterton
upheld, we fall into a kind of rationalistic insanity. Starving
the moral imagination (which must be nurtured early by

myth, fable, allegory, and parable), we find ourselves upon
the alienist's couch. Chesterton chose fantasy as his weapon
for defending common sense, knowing that defecated
rationality—private judgment carried to its extreme—is the
enemy of the higher reason.

"Every healthy person at some time must feed on fiction
as well as fact,"Chesterton puts it in his essay "Fiction
as Food," "because fact is a thing which the world gives
to him, whereas fiction is a thing he gives to the world.
It has nothing to do with a man being able to write; or
even with his being able to read. Perhaps its best period
is that of childhood, and what is called playing or pretending.
But it is still true when the child begins to read or sometimes
(heaven help him) to write. Anybody who remembers a
favorite fairy-story will have a strong sense of its original
solidity and richness and even definite detail; and will be
surprised, if he re-reads it in later life, to find how few
and bald were the words which his own imagination made
not only vivid but varied. And even the errand-boy who
read hundreds of penny-dreadfuls, or the lady who read
hundreds of novels from the circulating library, were living
an imaginative life which did not come wholly from
without."

By imagination, high or low, the world is ruled; and
not by little tracts and pamphlets. So, though a tractarian
polemicist of the first rank, Chesterton set out to reinvigorate
the moral imagination through fable: by "supposal,"
creating a fiction to impart a moral. "It is only in our
exhausted and agnostic age," he wrote late in life, "that
the idea has been started that if one is moral one must
not be melodramatic." The Greeks, the medieval scholars,
the Protestant moralists, and the eighteenth-century rationalistic moralists all knew better. Fantastic melodrama—
from the shape-shifting of the gigantic being called Sunday
(Nature incarnate) to the purposeful groping of Father

35

Brown—was Chesterton's instrument for the recovery of moral order. And of melodramatic subjects, none is more compelling than the madman and the madhouse.

In his **Autobiography**, Chesterton describes himself as a young lunatic at the time his first romance, **The Napoleon of Notting Hill**, was taking form in his mind. That madness of his, he writes, "was more and more moving in the direction of some vague and visionary revolt against the prosaic flatness of a nineteenth-century city and civilization. . . ." Only the humorist is sane, Auberon Quin declares in that novel (published in 1904). Quin gets up a comic scheme for restoring to the districts of London a medieval picturesqueness and a medieval autonomy. An heroic fanatic, Adam Wayne, takes Quin literally; loving Notting Hill, the little platoon he belongs to, he defends Pump Street, with swords and halberds, against all the forces of progress; and for twenty years he succeeds, though pulled down at last.

"This man Wayne," says Buck, one of Wayne's enemies, "would be shut up by any doctors in England." But is Buck himself less crazy than the Napoleon of Notting Hill? "Buck is mad," Quin observes, "because he cares for money, as mad as a man who lives on opium."

The satirist and the fanatic, Quin and Wayne, come to understand at the end that the two of them are mad—but only because they are two lobes of a brain that had been riven in two. "When dark and dreary days come, you and I are necessary, the pure fanatic, the pure satirist. We have between us remedied a great wrong. We have lifted the modern cities into that poetry which everyone who knows mankind knows to be immeasurably more common than the commonplace."

This high hope for reuniting the halves of the riven modern mind runs through the second of Chesterton's romances, too. "A Nightmare" is the sub-title of **The Man Who Was Thursday** (1908); but though the characters of that romance are sufficiently melodramatic, they are not mad. The one genuine anarchist among those seven conspirators is as rational as George Bernard Shaw. From the money-grubbing opportunist and the death-intoxicated anarchist, the time may be redeemed by common sense, poetic insights, and a touch of wit.

Yet by 1910, when he published **What's Wrong with the World** (a tract now almost forgotten), Chesterton began to suspect that the social order was sinking into insanity; it was becoming a tremendous madhouse, with scoundrels as the keepers. So it is that lunacy, and good men falsely accused of madness, peer out of his fantasies from **The Ball and the Cross** (1910) down to **Four Faultless Felons** (1930). In 1910, too, he wrote in his **Alarms and Discursions** that he was a sculptor of gargoyles: "These monsters are meant for the gargoyles of a definite cathedral. I have to carve the gargoyles, because I can carve nothing else; I leave to others the angels and the arches and the spires. But I am very sure of the style of the architecture and of the consecration of the church."

St. Paul's is the cathedral of **The Ball and the Cross**. In this madhouse fable, two of the gargoyles are Maclan, Jacobite and Papist; and Turnbull, militant atheist. The unreasonable cross surmounting St. Paul's is in danger of being overthrown by Professor Lucifer. Ours being an age of masks and conventions merely, this time is ripe for the Prince of This World; while belief endures only in a surviving saint, the monk Michael, and in these two honest opposed zealots, who cross swords literally as they flee from the indignant police.

That long pursuit terminates in a vast country-house lunatic-asylum, to which Lucifer—with the assistance of the civil authorities—has confined Michael, Maclan, Turnbull, and all casual witnesses of the combats between Highland Catholic and London atheist. Those two men scandalously believe that religion is worth fighting about; and so long as they remain at liberty, Lucifer's consummate rationalism cannot triumph. The very memory of burning faith must be immured in the deepest cells of the asylum.

Nevertheless the madhouse, a complex machine, suffers from any machine's ineluctable imperfections. Hopeful still, Maclan and Turnbull escape from the depths. Michael, the seeming imbecile (who has touches of the saint of Assisi), is unassailable in his wisdom, though members of parliament and magistrates are deluded by Lucifer. The asylum takes fire; Michael walks scatheless through the flames; and the asylum's master, Lucifer, hastens away in his flying-machine, casting overboard the doctors who were his tools.

One may note here similarities to C. S. Lewis' **That Hideous Strength**; both Chesterton and Lewis were influenced early by George Macdonald's fantasies. And there occurs a foretaste of Orwell—despite Orwell's lack of affection for Chesterton—in the final bland address of the Master to his captives:

"We investigated, on scientific principles, the story of Maclan's challenge, and we are happy to be able to inform you that the whole story of the attempted duel is a fable. There never was any challenge. There never was any man named Maclan. It is a melodramatic myth, like Calvary. . . . The whole story of the Maclan challenge has been found to originate in the obsessions of a few pathological types, who are now all fortunately in our care."

Yet patients sometimes set asylums afire; and in the ashes of this madhouse, there are found the swords of the two men of belief, "fallen haphazard in the pattern of a cross." The Ball and the Cross are not cast down.

From the dome of St. Paul's, Chesterton descended to the lodging-house of **Manalive** (1911). Innocent Smith, a towering humorist with a knack for reminding people of the joy of life—if need be, at pistol-point—comes under the observation of two doctors who think that he ought to be committed to an asylum. But in the mock trial of Smith, it is revealed that "his eccentricities sprang from a static fact of faith, in itself mystical, and even childlike and Christian." He is alive; while the doctors who would lock him up are dry sticks. Smith makes playful war upon defecated rationality.

"At certain strange epochs," Smith tells a curate, "it is necessary to have another kind of priests, called poets, actually to remind men that they are not dead yet. The intellectuals among whom I moved were not even alive enough to fear death. They hadn't blood enough in them to be cowards. Until a pistol barrel was poked under their very noses they never even knew they had been born. For ages looking up an eternal perspective it might be true that life is a learning to die. But for these little white rats it was just as true that death was their only chance of learning to live."

In **The Flying Inn** (1914), the regenerating poets are an adventurer and an innkeeper, Captain Dalroy and Humphrey Pump, who had rather see England drunk and free than sober and servile. This is perhaps the cleverest of Chesterton's moral melodramas, an assault upon prohibitionists, vegetarians, and all enemies of custom and common sense. Its rationalistic madman is Lord Ivywood—who, except for his manners, is Hitler, foreseen a generation early. Ivywood's fanatical pleasure in the breaking of bottles and the smashing of casks—"the pleasure which his strange, cold, courageous nature could not get from food or wine or woman"—leads to apostasy, a harem, and treason.

"I have gone where God has never dared to go," says Ivywood, at the moment of his ruin. "I am above the silly Supermen as they are above mere men. Where I walk in the heavens, no man has walked before me; and I am alone in the garden. All this passing about me is like the lonely plucking of garden flowers. I will have this blossom; I will have that. . . ."

By this fault fell the angels. The lust to reign in solitude, usurping the throne of God: this is the consummate madness, to cry "I am, and none else before me." The solipsist is the maddest, and most terrifying, of lunatics—and necessarily the worst enemy of both flesh and spirit. This illusion is "The Mirror of Madmen" in Chesterton's first book of serious poems, **The Wild Knight** (1900):

> I dreamed a dream of heaven, white as frost,
> The splendid stillness of a living host;
> Vast choirs of upturned faces, line o'er line.
> Then my blood froze, for every face was mine.

For the decade following **The Flying Inn**, the image of the madhouse was absent from Chesterton's writing. Those were the years of the War (from which Chesterton's spirits never wholly recovered), of the War's dreary aftermath, and of his conversion to Catholicism. Also they were years during which his Distributism struggled vainly against unprincipled consolidation and against socialist ideology.

Yet Chesterton did not despair. In 1925, he published **The Everlasting Man**; in the same year, **Tales of the Long Bow**. That romance of a hard fight against the political and commercial despoilers of England (a winning fight, unlike Chesterton's own real struggle) contains a passage describing the forces that Chesterton detested. Owen Hood sees his favorite reach of the rural Thames made hideous by a factory, and the river polluted by chemical wastes:

This was the beginning of what was for Owen Hood a crawling nightmare. The change advanced slowly, by a process covering years, but it seemed to him all the time that he was helpless and paralyzed in its presence, precisely as a man is paralyzed in an actual nightmare. He laughed with an almost horrible laughter to think that a man in a modern society is supposed to be master of his fate and free to pursue his pleasures; when he has not power to prevent the daylight he looks on from being darkened, or the air he breathes from being turned to poison, or the silence that is his full possession from being shaken with the cacophony of hell.

At once mover and toady in this devastation, Dr. Horace Hunter—presently knighted—is ready to certify as mad those who deviate from the dogmas of scientism. Professor Green delivers an impassioned and very odd address to a congress of astronomers; the trouble with Professor Green is that he has fallen in love. As a newspaper reports—

No less a person that Sir Horace Hunter, who, although best known as a psycho-physiologist, has taken all knowledge for his province, and was present to show his interest in astronomical progress, was able to certify on the spot that the unfortunate Green was clearly suffering from dementia, which was immediately corroborated by a local doctor, so that the unhappy man might be removed without further scandal.

Professor Green is forcibly rescued by an aviator, who spirits him away to the sanctuary and stronghold of the rebels against utilitarian and profiteering oligarchy. The League of the Long Bow, which in the end overcomes the despoilers (as much by mirth as by force), is led by lovers; while the politicians and industrialists are men of appetite only.

In the real England of those years, the Distributists enjoyed no successes like those of the League of the Long Bow. In 1927, with employment growing and the Depression settling upon the face of Britain, Chesterton published **The**

Return of Don Quixote. Herne, librarian at a country house, is obsessed by medieval studies, and is made King at Arms in a new order; for there is something of the prophet in him, and he is fearless. Sick at heart in his hour of victory, however, he casts off his own aristocratic supporters and comes to wander the roads after the fashion of Quixote, because he cannot ignore the injustice done to Dr. Hendry, the inventor of Hendry's Illumination Colors, by the monopolists of the paint-market.

Hendry very nearly is thrust into a madhouse by a new commission empowered to commit inefficient folk to protective custody. For Hendry expounds a curious theory of color-blindness, to account for his ruin at the hands of the monopolists; and such foolishness is anathema to Dr. Gambrel, an agent of the commission. (Gambrel rejoices in his own peculiar theory of Spinal Repulsion, tracing "brain trouble in all those who sat on the edges of chairs, as Hendry did.") Gambrel drags Hendry to a magistrate of the Lunacy Commission:

"Dr. Gambrel had the power of the modern state, which is perhaps greater than that of any state, at least so far as the departments over which it ranges are concerned. He had the power to invade this house and break up this family and do what he liked with this member of it. . . ." The examination of Hendry is conducted in a private house.

> For the policy of all recent legislations and customs had been in the direction of conducting public affairs in private. The official was all the more omnipotent because he was always in plain clothes. It was possible to take people to and from such a place without any particular show of violence; merely because everybody knew that violence would be useless. The doctor had grown quite accustomed to taking his mad patients casually in a cab; and they seldom made any difficulty about it. They were not so mad as that.

Through the contrivance of a waggish knight-errant, the magistrate is misled to take Hendry for the alienist and

Gambrel for the madman; Hendry goes free. For "Monkey" Murrel, Hendry's rescuer, "the real story lay rather in front of him than behind him; as if the unexpected liberation of the poor old crank, with the color-blind monomania, were but a symbol of the liberation of many things and the opening of a brighter world. Something had snapped; if it was only a bit of red tape; and he did not know yet how much had been set free."

Chesterton's own ride as Quixote was of small avail against the red tape of bureaucracy and oligopoly, during the Twenties. But he smote hard. In her biography of Chesterton, Maisie Ward does not mention **The Poet and the Lunatics** (1929). Yet I rate that series of fantastic tales high in Chesterton's fiction.

Gabriel Gale, its intuitive hero, has a talent for mollifying madmen and moderating their excesses. The whole book is about lunacy and its subtle causes in this century.

"Genius oughtn't to be eccentric!" Gale exclaims. "Genius ought to be centric. It ought to be the core of the cosmos, not on the revolving edges. People seem to think it a compliment to accuse one of being an outsider, and to talk about the eccentricities of genius. What would they think if I said I only wish to God I had the centricities of genius?"

The maddest of all maniacs is the man of business, as Gale discovers from a considerable acquaintance among madmen. Also there is the Russian psychologist who believes in emancipation, expansion, the elimination of limits: he begins by liberating a caged bird (to its destruction), next frees goldfish from their bowl, and ends by blowing up himself and the house where he has been a guest.

"What exactly is liberty?" Gale inquires, just before the explosion. "First and foremost, surely, it is the power of a thing to be itself. In some ways the yellow bird was free in the cage. . . . We are limited by our brains and bodies; and if we break out, we cease to be ourselves, and, perhaps, to be anything. . . .

"The lunatic is he who loses his way and cannot return. Now, almost before my eyes, this man had made a great stride from liberty to lunacy. The man who opened the bird-cage loved freedom; possibly too much; certainly very much. But the man who broke the bowl merely because he thought it a prison for the fish, when it was their only possible house of life—that man was already outside the world of reason, raging with a desire to be outside of everything." The Russian psychologist could not endure the "round prison" of the overarching sky: but his alternative was annihilation, and he chose it.

In these stories, one encounters the scientific maniac, purged of conscience, ready to kill for the sake of a museum's endowment; the artistic maniac, murderous when disabused of his pet fallacy; the anti-superstition maniac, more fanatical than any witch-doctor. One encounters, again, the solipsist who begins to fancy that he is God, and who can be saved only through intense pain:

"There is no cure for that nightmare of omnipotence except pain; because that is the thing a man **knows** he would not tolerate if he could really control it. A man must be in some place from which he would certainly escape if he could, if he is really to realize that all things do not come from within. I doubt whether any of our action is really anything but an allegory. I doubt whether any truth can be told except in a parable."

Therefore Gale pinned a poor self-intoxicated curate to a tree during a fierce storm, until the man recognized his own puniness, and that he was not sitting in the sky, and that he had no angelic servants going "to and fro in colored garments of cloud and flame and the pageant of the seasons." Lacking forcible parables, we are swallowed up by the monstrous ego.

Because he ridiculed certain powerful interests, Gale himself escapes being committed to a madhouse only through liberation by an armed genuine lunatic. The corrupt and treacherous psychologists who would put Gale behind walls tell him that he is a megalomaniac expressing himself in exaggeration. He has painted huge sardonic caricatures; and so—

> "You cannot see a large blank wall without having an uncontrollable appetite for covering it with large pictures," the malicious Dr. Wolfe tells Gale. "You cannot see a swing hung in the air without thinking of flying ships careening through the air. I will venture to guess that you never see a cat without thinking of a tiger or a lizard without thinking of a dragon."

True enough, Gale replies; but the trouble with his captors is that they cannot perceive essences:

> Psychology is certainly valuable. It seems to teach us how to see into each other's minds. You, for instance, have a mind which is very interesting; you have reached a condition which I think I recognize. You are in that particular attitude in which the subject, when he thinks of anything, never thinks of the centre of anything. You see only edges eaten away. Your malady is the opposite to mine, to which you call making a tiger out of a cat, or what some call making a mountain out of a molehill. You do not go on and make the cat more of a cat; you are always trying to work back and prove that it is less than a cat; that it is a defective cat or a mentally deficient cat. But a cat is a cat; that is the supreme sanity which is so thickly clouded in your mind. After all, a molehill is a hill and a mountain is a hill. But you have got into the state of the mad queen, who said she knew hills compared with which this was a valley. You can't grasp the thing called a thing. Nothing for you has a central stalk of sanity. There is no core to your cosmos. Your trouble begins with being an atheist. . . .

I know what is at the back of your mind, Dr. Simeon Wolfe; and it's a chaos of exceptions with no rule. You could find anything abnormal, because you have no normal. You could find anybody mad; and as for why you specially want to find me mad—why, that is another disadvantage of being an atheist.

At the end of **The Poet and the Lunatics**, the more criminal of these two mad-doctors has set up a private asylum in Wimbledon, its garden very like the splendid grounds of the madhouse in **The Ball and the Cross**. But the pretended patients are not mad at all: they are professional criminals, Dr. Starkey's agents, feigning insanity to gain immunity from prosecution. Somewhat as Chesterton the journalist found out rascals in high political places, Gale finds out Dr. Starkey and his crew. But Chesterton's flesh-and-blood adversaries did not go to prison; they proceeded to higher honors and emoluments, most of them.

The novelettes of **Four Faultless Felons** (1930) contain Chesterton's last studies in lunacy. "The Moderate Murderer" has a religious maniac for a foil, and a homicidal builder of empire who is madder and more dangerous. Hume, a dominie, averts the assassination of the Governor of Polybia by interrupting the Governor's stroll—his instrument of interruption, in the emergency, being a bullet through the Governor's leg. Had the Governor continued his walk, he would have been killed on the rifle-range by the no-nonsense-with-natives Deputy Governor.

"You once told me you feared for your family sanity," says the sharpshooting Hume to his sweetheart, "merely because you had bad dreams and brooded over things of your own imagination. Believe me, it's not the imaginative people who become insane. It's not they who are mad, even when they are morbid. They can always be woken up from bad dreams by broader prospects and brighter visions—because they are imaginative. The men who go mad are unimaginative. The stubborn stoical men who had only room for one idea and take it literally. The sort of man who seems to be silent but stuffed to bursting, congested—."

In the same volume, "The Honest Quack," a Dr. Judson, endeavors to commit his friend Walter Windrush to an asylum, that he may save him from a charge of murder. Judson concocts a Theory of Arboreal Ambidexterity, expressly to prove that Windrush (whose life centers round a rare tree he guards in his walled garden) is an anthropoid sport, not responsible for his own actions, because suffering from the rare mental affliction of Duodiapsychosis.

> The result, went on the doctor, the really dangerous result, lies in a tendency to separation between the functions. Such ambidexterity is not natural to man in his existing evolutionary stage and may lead to a schism between the lobes of of the brain. One part of the mind may become unconscious of what is attempted by the other part. . . . The attempt to render the variation of branches by simultaneous ambidextrous action leads to a dissociation of cerebral unity and continuity, a breach of responsible moral control and coordinated consecutive conservation—.

To obtain a colleague for committing Windrush, Dr. Judson successfully butters up that whited sepulchre Dr. Doone, the high authority on Arboreal Man, who signs the document of committal. After all, though, Windrush is found innocent by the police, and the real murderer takes poison—Dr. Doone himself. Walter Windrush is restored to his guardianship of the unique sprawling tree—under which, unknown to him, a murdered man's bones had lain for many a year. Dr. Judson wonders how Windrush can bear dwelling beside the tree now.

"My dear fellow, and you are the cold and rational man of science," said Windrush lightly. "In what superstitions you wallow! In what medieval darkness you brood all your days! I am only a poor, impracticable, poetic dreamer, but I assure you I am in broad daylight. In fact, I have never been out of it, not even when you put me in that pleasant little sanatorium for a day or two. I was quite happy there, and as for the lunatics, well I came to the conclusion that they were rather saner than my friends outside."

Privately, Windrush really believes that the garden of his Tree is the Garden of Eden; and he is not wrong. The skeptical Judson and his love Enid Windrush discover it for themselves:

> On top of the once accursed tree a small bird burst into song, and at the same moment a great morning wind from the south rushed upon the garden, bending all its shrubs and bushes and seeming, as does the air when it passes over sunlit foliage, to drive the sunshine before it in mighty waves. And it seemed to both of them that something had been broken or been loosened, a last bond with chaos and the night, a last strand of the net of some resisting Nothing that obstructs Creation, and God had made a new garden and they stood alive on the first foundations of the world.

Gardens are what men make of them. Maclan and Turnbull, entrapped, found themselves in the apocalyptic garden of Professor Lucifer's madhouse; Judson and Enid found themselves the new Adam and Eve, in the first of all gardens. And Chesterton, like Owen Hood, was resolved that some private gardens must endure. Wrath against the sophisters of lunacy—those pairs of cunning doctors committing sane men to Bedlam—runs through these stories: wrath against the devastators of gardens.

I do not suppose that Chesterton entertained any special animosity against doctors generally; rather, the mad-doctors of his parables stand for defecated intellectuality in our time—for the cult of Rationalism leagued with the selfish and domineering appetites of men emancipated from old obligations and loyalties. To his literary opponents, notably Wells and Shaw, Chesterton was polite and even kindly when he met them—being mindful, perhaps, of Augustine's injunction to hate the sin but to love the sinner. His dealings with alienists were similar; indeed, he found at least one admirer among their number.

One of the few people who ever apprehended **The Man Who Was Thursday**, Chesterton tells us in his **Autobiography**, was a French psychoanalyst. "He made my hair stand on end by saying that he had found my very juvenile story useful as a corrective among his morbid patients; especially the process by which each of the diabolical anarchs turns out to be a good citizen in disguise. 'I know a number of men who nearly went mad,' he said quite gravely, 'but were saved because they had really understood **The Man Who Was Thursday**.' "

The world is not evil; most men, of whatever profession, mean no mischief; delusion, rather than malice, is the curse of our time, ordinarily. Yet behind the arrogance of twentieth-century intellectuality, Chesterton believed, there works a corrupting power that is not merely human. That same power employs the consuming selfishness of the monopolist, the strutting **libido dominandi** of the unprincipled politician, the gnawing envy of the ideologue. Detesting sanity, this power whispers to men that they may be as gods—and draws them within the walls of the madhouse.

Every private garden—the gardens of the spirit, the gardens of the peasant—would be scorched to death by this power. And when this power cannot delude, it operates through human pride and injustice and violence to over-whelm those sane men who continue to resist. Such is the power described in the king's vision of **The Ballad of the White Horse**:

> The wise men know what wicked things
>   Are written on the sky,
> They trim sad lamps, they touch sad strings,
> Hearing the heavy purple wings,
> Where the forgotten seraph kings
>   Still plot how God shall die.

Those melancholy wise men are of the East; but the Christian, whatever his strength of reason, knows that he cannot know whether he will fail or win; he goes gaily in the dark, unsure of the end. Night is thrice night over him, in this time as in King Alfred's: the enemies of nature are grown subtle and ruthless. Anarchist and tyrant, positivist and technologist, fraudulent psychologist and avaricious oligopolist, undertake his ruin.

Unreason and Devastation are the stony idols of these enemies, and before them the modern crowd bows down. Unreason may seem fashionably clever, and Devastation has its charms for the bored and the hopeless. Huddled in a corner of his scientistic cell, often the lunatic detests the light—and would shriek, were he thrust into the sunny garden. It is not Dr. Dryasdust who can rescue the mad man and nurture the gardens of this world; prosy literalness, however well intentioned, cannot redeem the time; in the phrase of Disraeli, "Even Mormon counts more votaries than Bentham." If we are to be redeemed at all, we must be saved by the moral imagination, rising out of the historical consciousness (the work of **The Everlasting Man**) and out of the transcendent truths of allegory.

If all of our actions are allegories, men may apprehend reality only through parables. Of possible parables, Chesterton—he being sane and free—was haunted by the parable of the confining madhouse, and by the opposed parable of the garden. The madhouse is sterile, the prison of the solipsist; the garden, proliferating, expresses an immortal continuity and community, realized in time and place. If we burst out of the garden, we burst into the madhouse.

Innocent Smith, in **Manalive**, makes his way afoot quite round the world, that he may come afresh to wife and children and house and garden. "But don't you see," he shouts at a Russian station-master, "that all these real leaps and destructions and escapes are only attempts to get back to Eden—to something we have had, to something at least we have heard of? Don't you see one only breaks the fence or shoots the moon in order to get **home**?"

His Russian host doesn't see; and that blindness, Innocent retorts, is why the Russian Revolution has failed.

"I mean that if there be a house for me in heaven," Innocent Smith declares later in his travels, "it will either have a green lamp-post and a hedge, or something quite as positive and personal as a green lamp-post and a hedge. I mean that God bade me love one spot and serve it, and do all things however wild in praise of it, so that this one spot might be a witness against all the infinities and the sophistries; that Paradise is somewhere and not any-where, is something and not anything. And I would not be so very much surprised if the house in heaven had a real green lamp-post after all."

The real world, the world of sanity, the realm of centricity and common sense, is made known to us through parable; yet once known, it is a most substantial world, filled with small precious things infinitely dear to the sane man. Men deprived of their own lamp-posts may find other uses for lamp-posts; men whose hedges have been grubbed up may be cribbed, cabined, confined. The alternative to the little garden is the vast madhouse. G. K. Chesterton, decidedly a man alive, strove in parable to defend the hedges of that one spot which is Eden. If those hedges should be swept away, we would not find ourselves rejoiced by the elimination of limits. Instead, we should find ourselves bounded by the walls of that one spot, forever parched, which is Hell.

3

Chad Walsh

CHARLES WILLIAMS' NOVELS AND THE CONTEMPORARY MUTATION OF CONSCIOUSNESS

LITERARY HISTORY IS A TASTEFUL COLLECTION OF PROCRUSTEAN BEDS, arranged in convenient movements, periods, and centuries, and guaranteed to accommodate any dead author invited to find his resting place. A little stretching or lopping off of the corpse may be required to make a fit, but no matter.

A custom has grown up among those occasional and odd specialists who are interested in Christian faith and high imagination, of grouping Williams, Tolkien, and Lewis as a kind of literary Trinity. Already the revered images of Lewis and Williams, like skilled handiwork of Mme. Tussaud, rest in identical beds, and the very much living

Tolkien can glance over his shoulder and see the inviting—and identical—bed of immortality and scholarly footnotes waiting for him.*

In short, we can't escape using labels. At least we don't. We find what certain writers have in common and we create categories. I plead guilty with the rest. I, too, group Williams, Lewis, and Tolkien together, on the simple grounds that they share at least two things in common: Christianity and a soaring imagination. And, I might add, they often combine the two, though this is less obviously true for Tolkien than for Lewis and Williams.

If I were trying to set up certain distinctions, to discern not resemblances but differences in impact and flavor among the three authors, I would probably use the reading habits of college and university students as my litmus paper. On the basis of some haphazard snooping at college book stores and observation of the books that students bring to class along with assigned texts, I can make a preliminary report, none of which will contain any surprises. Tolkien easily leads the field. He had inherited the mantle that Golding with **Lord of the Flies** once wore, a mantle that had been passed to him by Salinger, author of **Catcher in the Rye**. Tolkien is what a student reads when he isn't reading something he has to read. Possibly the vogue has now pretty well worked its way down to high school and lower, sure indication that it will wane on the college campuses, but at any rate it has been an impressive phenomenon, and one worthy of a moment's speculation.

Tolkien's imagination, at once soaring and infinitely detailed, offers the reader another world that requires no

---

* Alas, I feel the cold winds of mortality as I reread this paragraph. Tolkien has now joined Williams and Lewis in death. My paper was written toward the end of the 60's. That period is also reflected in the frequent references to campus turmoil. I do not, however, recant what I said about the new consciousness. I think the present quiet on the campuses is less a return to the 50's than a temporary period of emotional exhaustion and gradual regrouping of new consciousness forces—somewhat chastened by recent and current history, it is true.

more than the assent of the imagination. Devout Roman Catholic though the author is, he does not issue explicit demands upon the religious will. His imaginary world, as has often been pointed out, has more of the somber grandeur of northern sagas than the disturbing challenge of a **Divine Comedy**, a **Paradise Lost**, or C. S. Lewis' **Great Divorce** and the **Narnia** stories. In reading Tolkien, one escapes from the flatly rational world of big business, big education, big army, big computers, and enters into a mythic universe with its own non-Euclidian logic. When you wish you can return, refreshed and happier, to your accustomed days and ways, to your job as junior executive in one of the better corporations, or assistant professor of English in a first-rate publish-or-perish university. In short, and I do not use the term pejoratively—rather the contrary—Tolkien offers an **escape** from a world whose flatness of spirit makes an occasional escape a psychological necessity and the highest wisdom.

Of the three authors, I believe Lewis would come next among college students. Some of them, a devout minority, treasure his books as the most lucid and winsome exposition of the Christian faith that they have come on. These students are thus the survivors of that much larger group of readers who during the believing late 40's and early 50's eagerly consumed many pounds of C. S. Lewis along with incredible tons of such bland purveyors of faith as Norman Vincent Peale. More numerous on most campuses are those who read Lewis as they might Tolkien, for his sheer imaginative power. They roam a mythic Venus or Mars by reading **Perelandra** and **Out of the Silent Planet**, and if their exploration brings them face to face with an eldil or Maleldil himself, they accept the alien beings as part of the total myth and do not typically take the meeting as a confrontation and demand upon their commitment. Even the Narnian books, surprisingly popular with adults, can be read as first-rate romances, the divine Aslan being accepted as one with the speaking beasts of fairy tales.

The difference with Charles Williams is that he cuts off the escape routes. In his novels—and I shall treat only them—he starts with the familiar, matter-of-fact world, and he never leaves it. Rather, he dramatizes another kind of world impinging on ordinary days, weaving in and out, creating Armageddons of confrontations and conflicts within the context of ordinary society. With Williams, it is not possible to say, "We are now on Mars, and different rules prevail here." His characters live in cities and suburbs like those we know, they marry and are given in marriage, they work sometimes for a living. They are part of the humdrum world until suddenly that other world stakes a claim in the midst. And even then, the ordinary world remains. Thus with Williams one does not escape to a different world, a new logic, but rather copes with strange powers and longings erupting within a completely familiar world. In consequence, it is next to impossible to concentrate on the two worlds separately. They are so intertwined that one cannot be observed without observing the other. And since the second world is profoundly shaped by Christian dogma and sensibility, the confrontation facing the reader is inescapable. He cannot pick and choose; he cannot enjoy a refreshing holiday from responsibility; rather he is challenged to face ultimate moral and religious choices as he vicariously experiences the conflicts of the characters in the story.

To say all this in another way, Williams is a very integral writer. His imagination and his religious faith are so mingled and merged that it is fruitless to attempt any analytic separation. One has the impression, uncanny at times, that he simply pictured what he himself saw. He seemingly saw a world in which the Nicene Creed operated as surely in human affairs as the law of gravitation. The feeling produced by his novels is that he has not replaced one reality with another, but simply forced our eyes wider open, so that reality becomes a bigger word, and we recognize what has been there all along, but unseen because of our poor vision.

It is no surprise then that Williams seems rarely read by college students—or anyone else. His demands are too severe. And yet—and perhaps this is the main point of my whole paper—he is in a curious way a forerunner of what is going on today among the young, preeminently in the United states, but to a large extent among the youth of the entire western or westernized world. Some day the young will discover that if they distrust the computer and believe in the "feeling intellect," Williams was there before them. But they will also discover that in another sense, he is ahead of them; that he has advanced from the overthrow of Aristotle's dessicated disciples into shadows of ecstasy, and come out on the other side where head and heart, soul and the central nervous system, are reconciled and wedded into a unified concept of humanhood. Perhaps he is little read by students because first they must catch up with him.

At this point I must turn briefly sociological, emphasizing the usual disclaimer that I have no scholarly credentials whatever for the task. I speak only as a teacher who finds the yearly parade of new students more interesting—and often more surprising—than the predictable alternation of the seasons.

The "silent generation" of the 1950's has mutated into the most vocal college generation of living memory. But what is it saying? Many things, as much by implication as by express statement. Beneath all the specific demands and condemnations, I think it is saying that the American way of life, as actually lived by their parents (the affluent as much as the poor) is an unattractive candidate for their heart-and-soul allegiance. This verdict comes from the gut as well as from the brain; in fact, it is more like the instinctive shudder of someone passing through a ghastly landscape than the syllogistic conclusion of a long chain of reasoning. The half articulate outcry seems to be for a new way of life, one that will be humanly, emotionally, physically more meaningful than the "up tight" value system of the still dominant White Anglo-Saxon Protestant code and creed.

A visceral reaction, then, is taking place against the feel of American life as it empirically exists, and as it is feelingly perceived by the young. In the process of rejection, of course, they brush aside history as irrelevant. The almost full employment of our economy, which seems still a divine miracle to the aging survivors of the Depression, is not hailed as anything to mention on Thanksgiving Day; it is taken for granted, just as no one runs to bear the news that the sun has risen again and on schedule.

The discontented young divide, in a rough and ready way, into what for lack of better terms I shall call the actives and the contemplatives. The former are much easier for my own generation to understand. They function in a long American tradition going back to the War of Independence itself, and including the Abolition movement, the women's rights crusades, labor union movements, and God help us, even the Prohibition crusade. The northern students who ten years ago went south and laid their bodies on the line in Civil Rights activities were actually pro-claiming their allegiance to one part of the American Dream—they were trying to make social reality conform more closely to the spirit of the Declaration of Independence, the Gettysburg address, the Constitution itself. In many ways they were traditionalists. And even today, when they move sometimes on a more revolutionary and violent course, and seek to bring the entire machinery of government, education and business to a grinding halt, so that out of the ruins a new and better society can arise, they are still in the great tradition of American radicalism; across the years, John Brown reaches hands to them.

The actives tend to be moral absolutists, in the sense that everything becomes a moral question. At my college, for instance, there is a key card system in the dormitories, and a small group of students has been skillfully sabotaging the system, on the grounds that any attempt to exclude the general community is an immoral exercise of class privilege. Thus a prudential question becomes a moral one. The zeal of the activists often becomes like that of religious zealots.

The contemplatives,[1] on the other hand, practice the strategy of retreat. They do their own thing in as much peace as possible. Sometimes they combine into the rudimentary society of people sharing the same pad, or create self-sustaining communes. But their stance toward the broader society is likely to be—"Why worry about it? It's dying anyway. Go your own way and pay no attention to it."

The contemplatives frequently signal their stance by long hair, beards, strange attire, sometimes extreme sales resistance to TV commercials on cosmetics and soap. These are the visible signs of the conventionally recognized Hippies, but several things must be said. One, that many students who shave daily and patronize the dry cleaner, are just as much inwardly alienated from the "system" as the visible Hippies, and may match them joint for joint, cube for cube. The other observation is that the bizarre appearance of many young people **is** indeed an important indication that something is astir. To this extent their worried parents and editorial viewers-with-alarm are right. When styles of clothing and personal appearance change drastically, it is usually a clear indication that the soul is undergoing an upheaval and transmutation.

On the deepest level, I believe that a genuine change of consciousness is taking place before our bewildered eyes, and that the actives, to some extent, and the contemplatives, to a greater extent, represent visible byproducts of that

1. Actives easily mutate into contemplatives and **vice versa**. Often a student who looks "like a typical Hippie" is deeply, sometimes violently, involved in social and political action.

change. Such fundamental transformations in the way life is felt and viewed are historical rarities; perhaps the trio of Socrates, Plato and Aristotle are the clearest example, when they pulled archaic Greece out of its traditional ways, screaming and brandishing bottles of hemlock extract, and set it on the path of logic, philosophy, and ultimately systems analysis.

I shall dogmatically set down what I believe to be some of the changes in consciousness that are taking place. And before I list them, let me pay tribute to Marshall McLuhan, who understands at least a few of them, which is more than most of us do. In particular, he perceives how technology can condition consciousness; that TV, for instance, leads to a simultaneity of perception, as opposed to the linear, logical progressions of the printed word.

My list would include:
(1) A revulsion against impersonality, excessive bigness, over-organization. Conversely, a new personalism. A desire to relate to other people in groups small enough to be meaningful; a quest for the "I-thou" relation and a refusal to settle for the "I-it" relation.

(2) A revulsion against every kind of code ethics. The conviction that morality has to be situational. This understanding can vary from the most extreme subjectivism— such as the argument that since Hitler was doing his thing, it was o.k.—to something approaching the position of those theologians advocating situational ethics—the establishment of one basic principle, usually love, as the yardstick, and judging every act by whether it maximizes or minimizes love.

(3) A revulsion against the tyranny of the brain and the operations of formal logic. There is the feeling that man has become a kind of monster, with the useful brain taking over almost the totality of his life, and relegating

the emotions and the sensations of the nerve ends to a debased status. The new sensibility has implicit in it a desire to educate the emotions and the body, to make both more accurate and sensitive, as the brain has been habitually educated. Hence the growing popularity of sensitivity groups, etc.

(4) A revulsion against the tyranny of time, both as it operates on the practical level—punching time clocks and getting term papers in on the assigned date—and also as the concept functions metaphysically.

(5) An almost complete indifference to the usual organized forms of religion, coupled with an intense religious or protoreligious quest. In its more extreme forms, this involves the use of drugs in the hope of mystical experience. It includes also the new interest in astrology, Tarot cards, the Book of Changes, witchcraft. It is an attempt to find a transpersonal reality immanent in the individual and the moment—the Atman, or at least a few spirits or ghosts.

(6) An intense and wistful interest in those peoples and cultures that in one way or another have escaped total domination by western modes of experience. Students turn to Zen Buddhism and the mysticism of India in the hope of finding, at the very least, a **different** sensibility, a fresh way of experiencing the familiar and understanding it. The strong interest that many white students have in Black consciousness movements is often twofold: a passion for justice, and also the hope that from the Blacks, who have maintained a culture of their own in their enclaves, they will learn the secret of a less inhibited, more intuitive life style.

(7) Finally, a radical revaluation of the work ethic. The activists revalue it by turning deaf ears on corporate recruiters in the spring of the senior year, and by seeking other types of work that seem inherently meaningful: social

61

work, teaching, VISTA, Peace Corps, being an artist or writer. The more radical contemplatives are less certain that work as such is meaningful. Life is being, rather than doing; work is something to which you submit occasionally for practical reasons, but it must never become the central thing.

It would be an oversimplification to summarize all this by saying that "archaic man" is being reborn before our amazed eyes, in the persons of our sons, daughters, and students. It would not be a complete untruth, however, to make the assertion. Something tribal is astir, a fresh recognition of the emotions, a diffused and sometime quite primitive religiosity, a groping for new and personalized types of community, a greater willingness to listen to folksinger and poet than to computer programmer and logician.

Still, one cannot say flatly and without footnotes that archaic man is being reborn just as he was three thousand years ago. Seeming repetitions of historical cycles always occur with a difference. To this extent, time is certainly real. If something resembling archaic man is striding the campuses, it is archaic man with a difference. For one thing, the very pharmaceuticals that he puchases in order to expand his consciousness come more often from the chemist's laboratory than from nature; LSD is more sought after than the bud of the peyote cactus. Perhaps a more accurate way of stating the mutation is to say that an increasing number of men and women are mastering the art of shifting the gears of consciousness as often as they choose. During the day they may be practical students, concentrating on the books or the laboratories; or they may be junior executives, computer programmers, other pillars and necessities of the System. But at certain times, maybe at night, on week-ends, or during vacation, they shift into their other consciousness, meditating over manuals of astrology or the newest edition of **I Ching**, or trying the latest pharmaceutical, or making love, or singing folksongs in a community of other singers. The principles of linear thought may sustain their practical role part of the day, and McLuhan's simultaneity of experience and consciousness prevail at other times. All this goes against the grain to tradition western man, who wants to bring every moment of his twenty-four hours into one intellectual system, so that in principle at least the same kind of thought suffices for meditating on the balance of trade and the incarnation of Jesus Christ. It is nonetheless what is happening.

Returning now to Charles Williams, his novels range in time of publication from **War in Heaven** (1930), to **All Hallows' Eve** (1945, the year of his death). Thus his last novel is now a quarter of a century old, and was written in the final days of World War II, just before the onset of the Cold War, and half a decade before the bland 1950's, with their tepid religiosity and general spirit of conformity. It is a quarter of a century that seems a full century to the soul. In that time the colonial world has for the most part freed itself, unrecognized colonies have revealed themselves in our midst—the Black subculture, the subculture of poverty—and the great revolutions of life style have transformed everything, the young most of all. I make these points to emphasize how remote, sociologically speaking, Williams is from what we see about us. The fact that his novels point in so many ways toward the present climate of the soul becomes the more remarkable.

Let me first illustrate this by looking at one of his least discussed novels, **Shadows of Ecstasy**. Published in 1933, a third of a century ago, it foreshadows the fascination and hope felt by many alienated Whites as they discover the existence of a separate Black culture. The plot deals with a mysterious uprising, as much religious as political, throughout Africa. European armies are put to rout, and soon African planes appear over London and African faces are mysteriously everywhere. A few quotations from the manifesto issued by the African leaders shows a startling resemblance to the attitudes found in those Whites, mostly young, affluent, and educated, who look for psychological renewal from the ghetto:

> In the name of the things that have been and are to be, willed and fated, in the name of the gods many and one, the Allied Supremacies of Africa, acting by the will and speaking by the voice of the High Executive, desire to communicate to the rest of the world the doctrine and purpose of the cause in which they are engaged. They announce their immediate purpose to be the freeing of the African continent from the government and occupation of the white race; their further purpose to be the restoration to mankind of powers which have been forgotten or neglected, and their direction to ends which have hitherto been unproclaimed. They announce their profound belief that, as to the European peoples in the past, so to themselves in the future the conscious leadership of mankind belongs. . . . The potentialities of that superiority do not attempt to deny the capacities of Europe in their own proper achievements. The High Executive of the African Allies desires, in its first public summons to the creative powers of the world, to honor the immortal finalities of the past. It salutes the intellect, the philosophies, the science, the innumerable patterns of Europe. But it asserts that the great age of intellect is done. . . . The prophets of Africa have seen that mankind must advance in the future by paths which the white peoples have neglected and to ends which they have not understood. Assured that at this time the whole process of change in mankind, generally known as evolution, is at a higher crisis than any since mankind first emerged from among the great beasts and knew himself; assured that by an equal emergence from intellectual preoccupations, the adepts of the new way have it in their power to lead, and all mankind has it in its power to follow, not certainly by the old habits of reason but by profounder experiments of passions, to the conquest of death in the renewed ecstasy of vivid experience; assured of these things the Allied Supremacies appeal to the whole world for belief and discipleship and devotion. (pp. 42-44) [2]

The plot soon thickens in typical Charles Williams style,

---

2. All page references are to the American editions published by Pellegrini & Cudahy.

as the events of world history, and the private dramas of individual choice, divide mankind into the followers of the new faith of intuition and ecstasy, and the supporters of the more or less rational status quo. The latter are represented by a rather unattractive and moralistic Yorkshire vicar, Ian Caithness, allied with a famous retired physician, Sir Bernard. The man in the middle is the young professor of English, Roger Ingram, haunted by the intuition that the poetry he passionately loves is vibrant with a power he has not yet been able to take into himself. Eventually, with the encouragement of his understanding wife, Isabel, he casts his lot with the devotees of feeling. The European leader of the new movement turns out to be Nigel Considine, who, it is revealed, is two hundred years old, having achieved this quasi-immortality by taking no sex and little food for two centuries, thus converting his passions into enduring life.

Eventually it appears that the movement is not authentically African at all, but rather a special kind of neo-colonialism. The long-lived Nigel Considine has been at work in Africa more than a century, preparing the way for the movement, and the African devotees are little more than his foolish tools. Considine finally meets his end through treachery from one of his European disciples, and the movement crumbles. The European armed forces restore order in Africa, and presumably rationality European-style prevails.

In this novel Williams ventured into very deep water indeed, no matter how disappointing and period-bound the ending may seem. He foresees with uncanny accuracy not just the fact that today many Whites are turning to their dark-skinned brothers for understanding of all that has been neglected and put to shame in the logic-dominated centuries, but also the diffused religious quality that envelopes the quest to know the dark depths of the living soul. Though none of the characters, so far as I can recall, takes drugs

as a means to this ecstatic knowledge, the stage is set
for whatever means might prove useful to discover a self
and a world beyond that revealed by the formal operations
of the scientific method and the procedures of systematic
logic.

One may ask—which side of the fence is Williams on?
In a way, on both. He recognizes the world of intuition
as a real world, and an immensely attractive one. When
forced to choose between such a world and the shallow
rationalism represented by the buffoonish prime minister,
the young English professor, who seems a central character,
opts for the luminous heart of darkness. On the other hand,
Williams seems to suggest that even in such a voyage of
exploration, it's a good idea to take your brains along.
Roger meditates at one point that mere belief in something
proves nothing: ". . . the fact that a supernatural hypothesis
had quite definite advantages didn't make it true. The fact
that man wanted a thing very much never would make
it true. . . ." (219)

Sir Richard, equally skeptical of Christianity and the
new paganism, reflects on the merits of rationality: "He
saw the intellect and logical reason of man no longer as
a sedate and necessary thing, but rather a narrow silver
bridge passing over an immense depth around the high
guarded entrance of which thronged clouds of angry and
malign presences. Often mistaking the causes and often
misjudging the effects of all mortal sequences, this capacity
of knowing cause and effect presented itself nevertheless
to him as the last stability of man. Always approaching
truth, it could never, he knew, **be** truth, for nothing can
be truth till it has become one with its object, and such
union it was not given to the intellect to achieve without
losing its own nature. But in its divine and abstract reflection
of the world, its passionless mirror of the holy law that
governed the world, not in experiments or ecstasies or
guesses, the supreme perfection of mortality moved. . . ."
(140)

The emphasis on intuition, passion, and ecstasy among the followers of Considine, the yearning toward primitivism, takes the reader into the familiar terrain of romanticism, including its frequent murkiness of detail. The novel goes farther, however, than depicting a wallowing in emotions. A strain of ascetism and discipline is portrayed in the person of Considine and some at least of his followers. They are seeking new sources of power as systematically as anyone trying to harness thermonuclear energy, and they have a clear aim, the overcoming of death itself. Thus the book moves into that territory where magic is one of the facts of life.

In some of Williams' other novels the paranormal is explored with a greater variety of astounding detail. One hardly knows what word to use in describing a realm of existence which is not necessarily more divine than common sense daily life, but one where strange things, with their own kind of logic, happen. For lack of a better term I shall use a colorless word and call it the preternatural. To Williams this is not a geographically or temporally separated world, but rather an ever present—or at least ever potential—dimension of ordinary existence. He seems to invite us to open our eyes a little wider and **really** look around—and see what we see. His attitude makes one think of Aldous Huxley's theory about the mechanism by which the psychedelic drugs operate. Huxley suggested that one of the functions of the brain is to strain the input of information, and that normally it allows only practical data to get inside the mind; drugs, therefore, are simply a means of putting the censoring machinery to sleep, so that reality in its fullness can flood in.

I wish to explore some of the features of Williams' landscape of the preternatural, or his understanding of the preternatural dimension—express it how you will. The novels are an anthology of specifics. Along the way I shall at times have some things to say about ways in which Williams' view of reality relates to the new consciousness that seems to be mutating into existence in the young.

The preternatural is, for Williams, a realm in which magic, both white and black, functions. Magic is not an ultimate power. In the realm of the preternatural, as in all realms, only divine power is ultimate. Magic is not so much viewed as grounded in the divine as in certain powers of man and nature that we habitually ignore, but which have their own precise laws. When Considine sets about to live forever, he becomes in his own way as ascetic as any early Christian hermit, and disciplines himself to focus his entire energy on one goal. The magician, Simon, of **All Hallows' Eve**, is another ascetic, who studies his diabolical craft as systematically as a scientist seeking secrets in the laboratory.

Magic is real, magic is powerful, but in Williamsland it is not ultimate. In a clearcut contest with spiritual power, mere magic loses. For instance, there is a scene in **War in Heaven** where the Holy Grail (which has been reposing in a country church) begins to quiver and dissolve. The archdeacon recognizes that enemies are bringing magic power to bear in an attempt to destroy the Grail. Hastily he organizes the little group about him into a prayer circle, and they match the power of prayer against the destructive spells of invisible magic. The archdeacon, being accustomed to prayer, provides the coordination for their effort, and it succeeds. The Grail is saved from the diabolic forces assailing it. In another novel, **The Greater Trumps**, a vast storm is magically created in England, and gets out of control. The world is threatened with a perpetual snowstorm. Normal human powers cannot stop it. But it is stopped by a young girl who, out of love, places herself in the path of the oncoming storm.

> . . . the warm hands of humanity in hers met the invasion and turned it. They moved gently over the storm; they moved as if in dancing ritual they answered the dancing monstrosi-

ties that opposed them. It was not a struggle but a harmony, yet a harmony that might at any moment have become a chaos. The column of whirling shapes arose and struck, and were beaten abroad under the influence of those extended palms, and fell in other whirling columns; and so the whole of the magical storm was sent pouring back into the place of its origin. (225)

The world of the preternatural therefore includes magic, but this is merely one aspect of it. Powers more directly related to the divine have the final say, once they go into action.

I sometimes wonder what Williams would say if he met a university student carrying an astrology book, a new edition of **The Book of Changes**, and a deck of Tarot cards. There would be, I imagine, a great deal of excited shoptalk, such as ensues, say, when two players of the Appalachian dulcimer happen to meet and discover their mutual hobby. The divergence might be on how to regard the preternatural. Perhaps the student treasures it for thrills or unusual experience. Williams sees it as part of the total reality, but always subject to the divine laws that govern every dimension or reality. Thus magic does not become a casual recreation. Rather, if one is to take it seriously, its inner principles must be soberly studied, and magic itself must be seen in relation to those spiritual laws which overarch it.

In the preternatural of Williams' novels the living and the dead coexist and sometimes meet, interacting upon one another. The heroine, Lester, of **All Hallows' Eve**, is killed by a disabled airplane before the story opens, and at first she thinks she is standing in her familiar London. Only gradually does she recognize that this is a different dimension of London; she is in the eternal London, not the empirical metropolis. Impelled by love and longing, she is able to make contact with her husband, and in fact her spiritual danger is that she will desperately seek to remain earthbound, instead of consenting to separation, and learning to explore the celestial London—which, however, is still related to the London that her living husband inhabits.

The communion and communication of the living and the dead in **All Hallows' Eve** are merely one aspect of something broader. Williams insists that distinctions of time are not ultimate; when they collide with eternity, the eternal now, it is the eternal now that wins. Thus it becomes possible for Williams in **Descent Into Hell** to dramatize his favorite doctrine of "substituted love" in two frameworks: one where normal time is still operative, and the other where the "eternal now" takes over. The first episode involves Pauline Anstruther, who lives in terror of her image, a doppelgänger that she sometimes sees coming toward her. The playwright, Peter Stanhope, who is deeply intuitive about these matters, offers to assume the burden of her fear. In his imagination he lives through the fullness of her terror, and since the burden is now on his back, it cannot be on hers.

Later, Pauline encounters her distant ancestor who was martyred at the stake during the reign of Bloody Mary. The legend has always been that he cried out with joy as the flames enveloped him. In her encounter, transcending and abolishing time and space, she meets him while he is awaiting execution. By taking his fear upon herself, she makes it possible for him to go fearless to the stake—many centuries ago.

The doctrine of substituted love is a specialized manifestation of Williams' doctrine of coinherence, his insistence that we actually are members one of another, and that any atomistic theory of individuality is an illusion. Coinherence is not an achievement but a given; it exists just as the coinherence of branches on a tree exists. I might suggest in passing that perhaps some of the Hippie communes, in a vague and unanalyzed way, reflect this same intuition. They are an attempt to create a type of community which is more than a rational table of organization; communities in which the words "I" and "Thou" are

meaningful, and the relation of one member to another
is one of sharing and bearing both joys and sorrows,
responsibilities and hopes.

On the perennial question of the road to divine knowledge,
Williams recognizes both the ascetic and the romantic paths.
The ascetic practicing the negation of images eliminates
one obstacle and distraction after another—even though from
another viewpoint they may be good and proper in other
contexts—and arrives at last in that blinding darkness where
only God is left.

Mainly, however, Williams is the specialist in the Way
of the Affirmation of Images. He found the pioneer theorist
in Dante, who had seen in Beatrice a stepping stone to
the knowledge of God. But anything can be the magic key.
In **Shadows of Ecstasy**, rather sluggish Philip suddenly looks
at the arm of his equally sluggish fiancee as she passes
a plate, and vistas of eternity open up:

> There was a line, a curved beauty, a thing that spoke to
> both mind and heart; a thing that was there forever. . . . And
> then as she stretched out her arm again he cried out that
> she was perfect, she was more than perfect; the movement
> of her arm was something frightfully important, and now it
> was gone. He had seen the verge of a great conclusion of
> mortal things and then it had vanished. Over that white curve
> he had looked into incredible space; abysses of intelligence
> lay behind it. (62)

Or take an episode from **War in Heaven** when the small
company of its defenders are gazing at the Holy Grail.
The Duke, scion of a long line of Roman Catholics, is moved
to think of martyred priests and secret masses, but finally—
"all these things, not so formulated but certainly there,
drew his mind into a vivid consciousness of all the royal
sacerdotal figures of the world adoring before his conse-
crated shrine. "Jesu, Rex et Sacerdos," he prayed . . ."
(152). The more prosaic archdeacon looks at the vessel and
murmurs, "Neither is this Thou, Yet this also is Thou."

71

With these words he distinguishes the image from the ultimate, but affirms the image as participating in the ultimate.

In certain respects, the Way of the Affirmation of Images is friendly to the secular city. It proclaims that the divine is knowable through anything and everything, provided that anything and everything are looked at from the right angle of vision. A filling station attendant putting eight gallons of high test into a tank becomes as much an imaging forth of the eternal activity in heaven's court as a priest solemnly going about the offering of the sacrifice of the mass. It is true, I think Williams would have insisted, that the mass has a certain priority, as a special channel of grace and means of communication created and blessed by God himself; perhaps for this reason, the divine is easier to recognize there than at the filling station. But by grace the moment in sight and insight can occur anywhere and any time, even in a filling station.

Thus it is that Williams takes the love of man and woman, the physical with the rest, seriously indeed, but not heavily indeed. He argues with some wit that you shouldn't try to pray and make love at the same time; the proper moods are different. But making love can be a mode of divine knowledge, for in the beloved one experiences some glimmers of the same love that prevails in the society of the Trinity and which brought into existence a universe where love is possible.

In all of these emphases, I think Williams has something in common with many of the trends of sensibility that one finds among the young. Certainly his insistence that what-ever is ultimate can reveal itself in bodies, ordinary cities, commonplace moments of life has a kinship with the insistence of the activists that man's proper job is in the world as it actually and visibly exists: that plain, ordinary social justice is more important, and more to be struggled for than transcendent goals directed toward another realm of existence. The vocabulary differs; the activist organizing a rent strike in the slums is not likely to speak of seeing the second person of the Trinity in the face of a mother or father of six undernourished children; yet, in his consciously secular way, he will be seeing what is ultimate to him, and in Williams' terms, that ultimate is the intelligent love that moves the sun and the other stars.

The Way of the Affirmation of Images also has some points of contact with the contemplatives, particularly as they strive to find in physical love and pharmaceuticals alternative routes to whatever is ultimate. In a curious way, the very fondness for "dirty language"—in particular those blunt, four-letter words that describe bodily functions— has about it something of the reverence for the created order that Williams extolls. True, dirty language may be used to shock the bourgeoisie and to display one's freedom from convention, but at the same time the words proclaim that either nothing physical is dirty, or everything physical is dirty. St. Peter, with his vision of all the forbidden beasts being offered him for food, might understand a Hippie who calls the act of sex or defecation by its plainest name.

Earlier in this lecture, I spoke of a "new consciousness" which seems to be emerging in some of the young, particularly those I called the contemplatives. It is interesting to observe that Williams' way of looking at the universe partly affirms and partly negates the new consciousness.

Williams' emphasis on hierarchy and formal courtesy is one of the prime conflicts. The great chain of being seems to be in the back of his mind. He finds an almost sensuous pleasure in describing a secretary who stands when her employer, a judge, stands, and who follows him through doors. It is as though the hierarchy of heaven, with its graded ranks of angels, is being imaged on earth. Courtesy in its more ceremonial and hierarchal forms is not an alluring virtue at the moment to those whose political, as well as social and spiritual thinking is based on "one man, one vote." In fact, the general concept of courtesy becomes equated with mere "good manners," and suggests yet one more hypocritical charade practiced by the uptight members of the Establishment.

Williams, however, is much closer to the new sensibility at several other points. His personalism, his emphasis on the living relation of human beings who are not mere squares on a table of organization, has many points of contact with the unrest sweeping the campuses. Williams has a vast theoretical substructure for his understanding of how human beings relate, but the goal he describes is close to what campus demonstrators mean when they symbolically burn IBM cards and agitate for smaller classes.

Close to the new consciousness also is Williams in his understanding of time. He is unwilling to grant that it is final. He grounds his conviction in the faith that all times are encompassed in God, and that the ever-present now of eternity makes travel between past, present and future a simple possibility and fact. The student contemplative may approach time more from the vantage point of Oriental mysticism, and simply experience its fading away as an illusion. In either case, the clock somehow becomes less of a final authority and arbiter.

Williams and the new contemplatives show deep interest in the preternatural. One of his novels is centered about the Tarot cards which are also an object of fascination to many students. The difference comes mainly in how one relates the preternatural to anything else. To Williams it is, so to speak, one dimension of the ordinary world, and if one is going to deal with it, he had best make a thorough study of the laws that govern its operation. Magic is no pastime for the amateur. But also to Williams, the preternatural lies under the divine sovereignty, and presumably to God it is just as matter-of-fact and "natural" as anything in ordinary, daily life. From Williams' view-point, a person who finds himself plunged into the realm of the preternatural need not change his values and orientation. If he has a relation to God, it still holds, and his job is to learn his way about in the preternatural, and function with the same motives and goals as before.

It is in the question of the rational mind that the most interesting agreement-and-conflict between Williams and the new contemplatives is revealed. They are in agreement in what one may call loosely the "romantic" way of looking at reality. They recognize the tidal depths of the emotions, the wisdom of the body, the possibility of magic and the depth of the preternatural realm. The parting of the ways comes in how all this is analyzed. Unless I am mistaken, many of the new contemplatives regard the reasoning mind as a sell-out. It has been corrupted by too many hours spent in the service of the System. It has been employed to perfect napalm, to promote the sale of useless products, to achieve Ph.D.'s by writing theses on worthless subjects. The mind, in short, has become a whore. Then down with the mind. Learn to think with your feeling, your body, your drugs. Reality will flood into you only as you silence the querulous quibbling of the mind. Therefore, the very effort to create an intellectual system whereby the preternatural can be seen in some larger context is a sell-out to the perfidious mind.

To Williams this is all a false dichotomy. The mind and the emotions alike are the invention of the one inventor. At their best, even the emotions partake of a rigorous and severe quality, rather than being a mere wallowing in sensation.

Williams has little patience for slipshod, self-deceiving thought. When the historian, Lawrence Wentworth, is rejected by a much younger woman, he sins against the factuality of reality by creating from his lustful imagination a facsimile of the lady which is pliant to all his desires. His descent downward into the hell of sustained illusions is aided also by his jealousy of a rival historian, and his failure to point out an error in costuming when asked his expert opinion concerning a play about to be produced. He has lost the good of the intellect, and the hell into which he descends affirms the loss.

Williams sees the universe as one universe, and finds in Christian dogma the keys to its architecture. Thus the realm of the preternatural is simply another province of man's homeland, not a foreign country. Thus also the ability of men quite literally to bear each other's burdens is not an isolated fact but a derivative of the primal bearing of burdens upon the Cross. The entire universe is theological through and through, and meaningful life consists of being caught up into that dance where the musician is the one who first created the dance.

The sense of the divine dance is so strong in Williams that it has literary consequences. His characters are believable enough, but not very individualized. We see enough of each to find it plausible when he turns toward the ultimate or rejects it. But we should not recognize many Williams characters if we met them in a secular drawing room. Their little peculiarities and idiosyncrasies are rarely mentioned. It is as though a divine light or a demonic light shines so brightly upon their faces that all accidental features are illumined out of existence.

Perhaps this is Williams' way of saying that there is only one story, one drama: the drama of movement toward love or toward the rejection of love. In their infinitely varied ways, Williams' characters move one way or the other, and the light upon their countenances—divine or demonic— countersigns their choices.

This, at least, is what remains strongest with me, as I finish re-exploring Williams' seven novels after some years of absence from them. I can testify that in many ways they seem more meaningful to me than when I first read them. The times have partly caught up with Williams. And partly, I think, he has outstripped the times. He has come out on the other side of our present confusions and agonies, and found that dimension of existence where intelligence and the heart serve each other, and where love is all the Hippies say it is because human love is never all there is.

4

Edmund Fuller

AFTER THE MOON LANDINGS: A FURTHER REPORT ON THE CHRISTIAN SPACEMAN C. S. LEWIS *

AS APOLLO 11 ENTERED THE FINAL STAGES OF COUNTDOWN FOR THE FIRST LANDING OF MEN ON THE MOON, in July of 1969, one man in all the swarm of correspondents reporting the event was troubled by doubts that seem to have bothered no other journalist, possibly to have bothered only one other person of any sort, present. One writer was asking himself, is the giant Saturn 5 vehicle "a potential chariot of Satan"?

That surprising person, accredited on this occasion as a reporter for LIFE magazine, was novelist, personal

---

* [Mr. Fuller's essay title alludes to his previous study, "The Christian Spaceman: C. S. Lewis," in his **Books with Men behind Them** (New York: Random House, 1962), pp. 143-68.—**Editor**.]

journalist, sometime New York City mayoral candidate,
film-maker, and self-styled "left conservative," Norman
Mailer.

He listened to press conferences of Wernher von Braun
and talked with him at a reception, reflecting: "He had
spent his life with the obsession of reaching other planets.
It is no small impulse. Immediate reflection must tell you
that a man who wishes to reach heavenly bodies is an
agent of the Lord or Mephisto."

Von Braun was that other person on the launch who
also had God on his mind, if not the Devil. At a banquet
the night before lift-off, the rocketeer had asserted to an
audience of businessmen and industrialists: "We are
expanding the mind of man. We are extending this God-
given brain and these God-given hands to their outermost
limits and in so doing all mankind will benefit. All mankind
will reap the harvest. . . ." And in a newspaper interview,
he had said, "Through a closer look at creation, we ought
to gain a better knowledge of the Creator."

Von Braun proceeded to still more explicit theological
speculations: "It could very well be that the Lord would . . .
send His Son to the other worlds to bring the gospel to
them—I believe the good Lord is full of such tremendous
compassion that He will take whatever steps are necessary
to bring the truth to His creation." Striking words on this
occasion from the mastermind of the huge space vehicle,
erstwhile rocketeer of Hitler's Third Reich.

Mailer, speaking in the persona of Aquarius, which he
had assumed for the occasion, explored his own thoughts,
past and present. "Once, tentatively, he too had undertaken
the doubtful liberty to state in an interview what he thought
of God. God, he had presumed to suggest, was an embattled
vision: God had created man in order that man might
fulfill God's vision, but His vision of the future was at

war with other visions of existence in the universe. Some
of those other visions were not only out in the stars, and
in the galaxies, but were right here, intimate, on earth.
God was, for instance, at war with the Devil. Certainly
the Devil had a most detailed vision of existence very much
opposed to His own. In any case the war had gone on
for so long that nearly everything human was inextricably
tangled. Heroism cohabited with technology. Was the Space
Program admirable or abominable? Did God voyage out
for NASA, or was the Devil our line-of-sight to the stars?"

After the awesome lift-off of Saturn V, the Rev. Ralph
Abernathy, who had led units of his Poor People's Crusade
to play the role of skeletons at this technological feast,
said, "This is really holy ground. And it will be more holy
once we feed the hungry, care for the sick, and provide
for those who do not have houses."

But Mailer-Aquarius did not feel certain about that,
either. "Aquarius was not yet ready to call this hallowed
ground. For all he knew, Saturn-Apollo was still a child
of the Devil. Yet if it was, then all philosophers flaming
in orbit, the Devil was beautiful indeed. Or rather, was
the Devil so beautiful because all of them, Johnsons, Gold-
waters, Paines, Abernathys, Press-Grubs and grubby
Aquarius, were nothing but devils themselves. For the notion
that man voyaged out to fulfill the desire of God was either
the heart of the vision, or anathema to that true angel
in Heaven they would violate by the fires of their ascent."
(LIFE, August 29, 1969.)

Von Braun called the moon launch "equal in importance
to that moment in evolution when aquatic life came crawling
up on the land. . . ." Mailer noted that the remark "passed
without pause over the birth and death of Christ"—to which
I would add, and over the resurrection. President Nixon
echoed Von Braun, in remarks at the splashdown, in terms
that made the omission still more noticeable. It would be

foolish, however, to attribute great significance to that. Either man surely would say that he was speaking within a human reference, not a divine one.

However, Mailer-Aquarius' blend of awe and misgiving at the moon launch must fascinate any close reader of C. S. Lewis' **Out of the Silent Planet** and **Perelandra**. Hastily, one adds that this is not because of literal correspondences, not to equate Von Braun with Lewis' Professor Weston, for example, or Mailer, even though one of Mailer's phrases, suggesting that God "was an embattled vision," is pure Westonese. Lewis' stories deal with many questions about man's purposes in space, the motives of his technological thrust, the complexities and ambiguities of all talk of God and Devil, and concepts of the nature of God and man.

Man's feat in actually landing on the moon and returning has already made oddly obsolete certain types of science-fiction which, until recently, seemed wildly ahead of their time. As I speak now, on this Nov. 19, 1969, they are there again—unanticipated by me as I planned this paper. The Mariner probes of Mars and Venus have destroyed the imaginative assumptions in many stories of voyages to those planets, abruptly reclassifying them from daring speculations to the quaint.

Some years ago I wrote a study of C. S. Lewis' fiction, called "The Christian Spaceman," in reference to his trilogy, **Out of the Silent Planet**, **Perelandra**, and **That Hideous Strength**, which involve journeys by his hero, Ransom, to Mars and Venus. Have the recent advances in the exploration of space destroyed the effectiveness of these stories?

Certainly not. Real technical achievement can have a damaging effect only upon that kind of science-fiction preoccupied largely with guessing the direction, devices, and pace of technology; "the fiction of engineers," Lewis called it. Even then, if the stories were any good, they may retain interest as part of the history of the imaginative extrapolation that races ahead of accomplishment by varying distances at different times. Lewis' stories are science-fiction only in the loosest usage. He preferred the less specific term "fantastic fiction." They are symbolic stories and technical developments do not invalidate them any more than, to modern Biblical scholarship, our knowledge of the vast age of the earth and of the evolutionary stages in man's development invalidate the great symbolic Creation stories of Genesis.

In one of the ebullient, off-the-cuff comments that made Nikita Sergeyevich Khrushchev so much more interesting than the dismal pack of **aparatchiki**—bureaucrats—who deposed him, he said that the Russian cosmonauts, in their early orbital flights, had not seen God out there. It was one of his sillier remarks, particularly for an eccentric Communist whose talk was irrepressibly laced with references to God.

But from the author of **Job**, to the Psalmist, and right on down to this moment, all sorts and conditions of men, believers, unbelievers, or agnostics, have been unable to separate thoughts of the solar system and interstellar space from thoughts of God, regardless of the enormous variation in what the word "God" means to them.

Time magazine, in the issue of January 4, 1969, under the heading, "Challenge in the Heavens," reported responses in theological terms to the Apollo 8 first manned journey around the moon. Theologians of several different church affiliations were quoted in concern—clearly premature—about the theological implications of the possible discovery of intelligent life elsewhere in space, and of man's possible encounters with and behavior toward such beings. A Roman Catholic chaplain at Edwards Air Force Base, in California, said that "theological think tanks" should be established to ponder such problems, and consulted the Rand Corporation about possibilities of a fellowship in space theology. I would be happier if the very concept and phrase, "think tank," did not remind me so forcefully of the NICE, Lewis' ironic acronym—ironic and prophetic—for the "National Institute of Co-ordinated Experiments"—an agency subverted to the Devil's work—in **That Hideous Strength**.

Again, **Time**, in the issue of September 5, 1969, under the heading, "Pop Theology: Those Gods from Outer Space," reports a new crop of books speculating on God, man, and space, including one by a German who finds the Old Testament to abound in what he interprets as visits to Earth by men from space. And a Russian—a **Soviet** Russian, mind you—propounds the view that Christ was a cosmonaut from Out There.

Of course, the movie **2001**, and the book of the same name which Arthur C. Clarke wrote to accompany it, and the story, **Childhood's End**, which was the earlier seed of the same tale, all are intensely mysterious, moving past the technological extrapolations and such persuasively amusing touches as the Pan Am flights to the moon and Howard Johnson's at the orbital station, to speculations on man's destiny. Clarke assigns visiting space men of an advanced order a role in the evolution of man. There is nothing explicitly theological in **2001**, and Clarke makes the point that where an enormous gap in cultures exists, technical achievement appears as magic to the less advanced culture, as rifles were magical killing sticks to Indians when they first saw them—a delusion that did not last long.

It is remarkable how fully C. S. Lewis anticipated and dealt with speculations of all these kinds. He remarked in a BBC broadcast conversation, which will be mentioned again later: "If you have a religion it must be cosmic; therefore it seems to me odd that this genre was so late in arriving." In 1958 he wrote for the **Christian Herald** an article called "Will We Lose God in Outer Space?", which later was incorporated into his book, **The World's**

Last Night and Other Essays (1960), under the chapter title, "Religion and Rocketry."

In that, in addition to warnings about man's probable behavior toward any alien life form he might encounter in space (warnings which will not be new to any readers of the **Silent Planet** trilogy) he makes one cautionary remark particularly important to us today:

> Each new discovery, even every new theory, is held at first to have the most wide-reaching theological and philosophical consequences. It is seized by unbelievers as the basis for a new attack on Christianity; it is often, and more embarrassingly, seized by injudicious believers as the basis for a new defence. But usually, when the Popular hubbub has subsided and the novelty has been chewed over by real theologians, real scientists and real philosophers, both sides find themselves pretty much where they were before. . . . Christians and their opponents again and again expect that some new discovery will either turn matters of faith into matters of knowledge or else reduce them to patent absurdities. But it has never happened. What we believe always remains intellectually possible; it never becomes intellectually compulsive. I have an idea that when this ceases to be so, the world will be ending.

I commend to you as of particular value for Lewis' comments on aspects of his own fantastic fiction, and his views about the genre at large, the posthumous collection, **Of Other Worlds: Essays and Stories** (1967), edited, with a Preface, by his secretary, Walter Hooper.

There, again with sound anticipation, Lewis himself makes it clear why the Mariner probes of Mars and Venus, which of course he did not live to see, do not invalidate the imaginative use he makes of those planets in **Out of the Silent Planet** and **Perelandra**. "In this kind of story the pseudo-scientific apparatus is to be taken simply as a 'machine' in the sense which that word bore for the Neo-Classical critics. The most superficial appearance of plausibility—the merest sop to our critical intellect—will do. I am inclined to think that frankly supernatural methods are best. I took a hero once to Mars in a space-ship, but when I knew better I had angels convey him to Venus. Nor need the strange worlds, when we get there, be at all strictly tied to scientific probabilities. It is their wonder, or beauty, or suggestiveness that matter. When I myself put canals on Mars I believe I already knew that better telescopes had dissipated that old optical delusion. The point was that they were part of the Martian myth as it already existed in the common mind."

On the other hand, as a great deal more knowledge of Mars and Venus is gathered—as our race becomes far more familiar with their features and characteristics—fantasists will seek new unknown realms for their stories. Indeed a vast amount of science-fiction has done so already. This is the principle which, from man's most ancient myth-making eras until now, has caused the imaginative story-teller to push farther and farther afield for his scenes. Lewis states the principle involved: "The less known the real world is, the more plausibly your marvels can be located near at hand. As the area of knowledge spreads, you need to go further afield: like a man moving his house further and further out into the country as the new building estates catch him up. Thus in Grimm's **Märchen**, stories told by peasants in wooded country, you need only walk an hour's journey into the next forest to find a home for your witch or ogre."

One of the current conjuring words is "relevance." If the fantastic fictions of C. S. Lewis are not obsolete because of the forward movement of technology, are they, in any case, "relevant"—and if so, relevant to what? That takes us back to where we started, to the fact that persons as disparate as Norman Mailer and Wernher von Braun both were impelled to talk of God in connection with man's first triumphant space voyages. What does that signify?

We are warned, not everyone who says "Lord, Lord"

shall enter into the Kingdom of Heaven. As Samuel Johnson remarked about patriotism, so too the name of God can be invoked as a last refuge by a scoundrel. Mailer, not necessarily impugning Von Braun, nevertheless observed justly that: "It was possible Von Braun was sincere. Still what a grip he had on the jugular of the closet missionary in every Wasp. If he had dumped his private finds on American religious opinion into a computer and cranked it up for response, the words could not have come back better."

Mailer's long-standing preoccupation with the idea of war between God and the Devil, cropping up in some very strange fictional contexts indeed in his novels, is one of the things that stamp his as an unusual mind in the orbit within which he moves. Of course the idea of that war in Heaven is ancient, with Biblical roots, and coming down through Western literature through Dante, Milton, Bunyan, Charles Williams, Tolkien, and C. S. Lewis, among others. But it is Lewis who puts it, however loosely, into a context of science, although he insists, properly, that investigational science is not at odds with religion, it is only scientism, the construction some men put upon science, that creates conflict. In **Perelandra** it is Professor Weston's philosophy, not his supposed scientific abilities, that serves the Devil.

What is fascinating is to find Mailer expressing belief in the contest between God and Devil. He is not a man with religious affiliations, Christian or Jewish. At times past he has been a spokesman of the Way Out, the hip as against the square. But among the diverse company he keeps—political, intellectual, artistic—his is the most religious nature, the most complex, the most interesting mind; also, the most perplexing and possibly dangerous.

I think he might willingly grant that in his speculations on the war between God and the Devil it is possible that he is not sure which side is which. Thus, even though I think he would like to side with God, he has a problem of identifying Him. This is quintessentially the **Perelandra** situation, and is what makes that book so dramatic and so unfadingly immediate. It has not diminished in value with progress in space exploration, it has increased. The technology has nothing to do with it, but the value questions have everything to do with it.

Mailer has never invoked this God-Devil conflict more aptly than in relation to the space program. Like all government activities, it is inextricably involved with, somewhat compromised and modified by, the Cold War, the space race as an aspect of Cold War, the political and prideful determination that the first man on the moon should be **our** man, By God!—And I confess I'm glad it was.—In short, it is inextricably involved with the nature of man, and man is fallen. A space ship is also a weapon carrier; a scientific research platform, in orbit or on the moon, is also a military base, all disclaimers notwithstanding. "One giant leap for mankind" can be toward the high country of Heaven or towards the abyss of Hell, just as much as the other part of Neil Armstrong's formulation, "One small step for a man" can be in either direction.

I know of no better place to which to refer this difficult question than to Chapter 7 of **Perelandra** in which Ransom's old antagonist from the first book of the trilogy, Professor Weston, now professes to be aligned in the same religious commitments and loyalties as Ransom. Instead of wishing to spread the domain and power of the human race, as before, he now asserts the aim to spread "spirituality." But under questioning, it proves that "spirituality" and "God"—a word which Weston prefers to evade—are radically different from Ransom's Christian definitions. Weston now proclaims himself a "chosen" man: "It is through me that Spirit itself is at this moment pushing on to its goal."

Ransom demurs: "Look here, one wants to be careful

about this sort of thing. There are spirits and spirits you know. . . . There's nothing specially fine about simply being a spirit. The Devil is a spirit."

The close-textured arguments in that Chapter 7, and the fierce debate in succeeding chapters to influence the choices that lie before the Green Lady, the Perelandrian Eve, are more relevant to the perplexing problems of purpose, loyalty, and choice for men in this dawning space age than anything else I know.

Do not suppose that my purpose, in all this, is complacently, securely, to warn Norman Mailer, or Wernher von Braun, of the perils of identification of sides, and of commitment, in the continuing war between God and the Devil. It is Edmund Fuller that I am warning, and you— each one of you—that I am warning. Seductions of the age beckon, abysses open, to each of us, as much or more to the confessed Christian believer as to the doubter.

One trap is the often heard notion that either a new religion, or a radical change in the old religion, is required in our time. This is dangerous ground, indeed, especially in the post-Vatican II ecumenical ferment, which is causing painful problems, particularly within the Roman Catholic Church, but all of which problems and phenomena of restlessness have counterparts in the other denominations or sects of Christendom.

It seems quite true that many young people are not reached by the conventional formulations of preaching and apologetics, or long-habituated patterns of worship and liturgy. The Sunday church service that seems a familiar comfort to many persons of fifty seems to say little, in a time of shattering changes, to some persons of fifteen. There is nothing inherently wrong, and may even be a merit, in speaking to persons of fifteen in terms different from those addressed to persons of fifty, in holding worship services with them in different ways, provided that the worship is unmistakably paid to the same God and within the terms of His own Scriptural instructions to us.

But one fashionable and ironic misdirection is away from mystery. We should not be shrinking from mystery, from what cannot be understood. A God who could be wholly understood would necessarily be an idol. I deplore the flight of several modern bishops of my own Episcopal Communion from the doctrine of the Trinity, for example. The Trinity is a mystery. The Creeds we say, whether the Apostles', the Athanasian, the Nicene, or the opening lines of the Gospel of St. John, are wholly mysterious. They are of Faith, not of demonstration. Why we should fear mystery in religion in an age when the most advanced probes of science reveal ever new mysteries in the universe of a stupendous scale, quite escapes me. It is a mistake, a confusion of categories, a loss of faith, a loss of nerve.

C. S. Lewis states often that his stories originated with pictures in his mind, not with an apologetical teaching intention. In a taped conversation with Kingsley Amis and Brian Aldiss, for BBC, included in **Of Other Worlds**, Aldiss says, "I would have thought that you constructed **Perelandra** for the didactic purpose." Lewis replied: "Yes, everyone thinks that. They are quite wrong. . . . I've never started from a message or a moral, have you? . . . The story itself should force its moral upon you. You find out what the moral is by writing the story."

Interesting as that is, nonetheless I think that fact may have led Lewis, so characteristically the scholar, the teacher, the don, to fail to realize that the messages and morals in his fictions, even though they did not directly motivate the writing of the fictions, nevertheless are more effectively communicated even than in his admirable didactic books. I think that long after such an excellent book as **Mere Christianity** is forgotten (and there are of course other such skillful apologetical works by other writers), that the **Silent Planet** trilogy, **The Screwtape Letters**, **The Great Divorce**, and his many other fantastic fictions (to which there are far fewer comparably good works by other writers) will be read and will continue to expound classical, orthodox Christian doctrine to minds that would never approach it, or open themselves to it, or understand it, in more formally didactic terms.

Apropos that, even the most so-called advanced study material perpared for Sunday School children that I have ever seen, is dreary, stale, flat, unprofitable stuff. I'd like to see it all thrown out and Christian doctrine introduced to the very young through the seven wonderful volumes of the **Chronicles of Narnia**, until somebody comes along with anything else as good or better.

I can give an odd backward compliment to that effectiveness. On the occasion of my second and last visit to Lewis, upon leaving I told him I was going directly to visit Professor Tolkien. Lewis laughed and said, "Don't talk to him about the Narnian books, he doesn't like them." I asked, "Why not?" Lewis said, "He thinks they're too explicit."

It's true that the Christian structure in them is more explicit than in **The Hobbit** or **The Lord of the Rings**, where it is present but deeply buried. Yet I believe that the relative explicitness of the Narnian books is a positive merit and value in them. It is not so clear that a completely uninstructed child would know it for what it is. But even for the uninstructed, it would lay down a foundation for understanding the Christian mystery in all its basic elements.

Lewis, by the way, was mildly annoyed by many people—Americans mostly, or entirely—who speak of the "Narnia books," or chronicles, instead of "Narnian," in the adjectival

form. He asked me, "Isn't the adjective known in America?"
I said, "Yes, but you should see what's happened to the
adverb!"

Lewis, of course, is not alone in his ability to communicate
Christian values, or doctrine, in terms that appeal to the
present-day consciousness, or by means of fantastic fiction.
J. R. R. Tolkien and Charles Williams, both of whom are
considered in this series of lectures, share that power in
their individual ways. My belief in the effectiveness of their
approaches has led me to write studies of some of the
work of each of them, as well as of Lewis. As I'm sure
you know, the three were friends, given at one of their
most productive periods, to reading aloud work-in-progress
together, cross-fertilizing one another's imaginations. I
should mention, also, Dorothy Sayers, who exhibits the same
gift in her splendid plays, especially in **The Zeal of Thy
House**. She was even able to extract comedy from the
Council of Nicea in **The Emperor Constantine**, in—of all
things—an inspired barbershop scene.

I strongly recommend to you a remarkable American
book, increasingly accepted as a classic of its genre (science-
fiction, or fantastic fiction): **A Canticle for Leibowitz**, by
Walter M. Miller, Jr. On the occasion of a visit with Lewis
in June of 1962, I had the pleasure of giving him a copy
of that book. In the Amis-Aldiss-Lewis conversation, which
occurred in December of 1962, Lewis was asked about it
and said in part, "It was a major work, certainly. . . . on
the whole it was well imagined and well executed." The
quality which leads me to urge it upon you as a worthy
American companion to the fiction of Lewis, Tolkien, and
Williams, is the depth and full dimensionality it achieves
by the fact that it may be said equally to use the future
of mankind to examine his past and present, or to use
his past and present to examine his future. It is at once
amusing, appalling, intellectually fascinating, and theologically sound—no mean achievement. I have found it an effec-

tive book for teaching. But aren't such stories "escape"? Quipped Tolkien to Lewis: "What group of men are most hostile to escape stories? Answer: jailers." Stories of this kind free the mind to roam. They provide far better trips than LSD!

Omitted from the mention a moment ago of other writers with the gift for encapsulating Christian doctrine within fantastic fiction, was the name of George Macdonald. That Victorian Scottish clergyman wrote several extraordinary and haunting tales of the supernatural and the land of Faerie. **Phantastes**, **Lilith**, **The Golden Key**, and the two Curdie books are the important ones.

Close reading of these and of the stories of Lewis, Tolkien and Williams will reveal influences exerted by the Scot upon all three of the later men. I cannot explore them here. Lewis especially has acknowledged lovingly his unique personal debt to Macdonald—who sowed the seed of his conversion experience. Several of the story devices in the Narnian books, particularly the techniques of passing from one dimension of being to another, are borrowed from Macdonald by adaptation. Lewis writes of the Scotsman and testifies to this influence in the autobiography of his early years, **Surprised by Joy**, and in the Introduction to his small anthology of selections from Macdonald's writings other than the fantasies. Most important of all, he has used the incorruptibly-raised George Macdonald as his mentor in his dream vision of Heaven and Hell, **The Great Divorce**. This is one of Lewis's finest books, perhaps a little over-shadowed by the popularity of his other fiction. It must not be neglected. Its images of the meaning underlying the prayerbook phrase to "grow in the knowledge and love of God," which we petition for the souls of the departed, is as strong as anything Lewis has done.

By analogy, Lewis' fantastic fictions, in their totality, make it possible for him to be mentor to us, in the spiritual-theological perplexities of this technological-biological-nuclear-space age. He could not foresee the precise shape of the problems, but his guidelines—which simply means his clarifying presentation of Christian guidelines—will serve us well.

A word about the man. It would have been understandable that the news of his death was slightly overshadowed in the press by the death on the same day of Aldous Huxley. The fact was, of course, that both writers received obituary attention the more remarkable for its prominence because both died on the day of the assassination of President Kennedy. As a long-time admirer of Aldous Huxley, I will yet risk the guess that more of Lewis' body of work may last, and last longer, than Huxley's—a guess that might be scoffed at in literary media.

Those who knew Lewis well loved him. His intimates called him "Jack." It was not my privilege to know him closely—when I met him he was already a dying man. Chad Walsh, one of the lecturers in this series, knew him well over a long period of time.

But even my encounters gave me the flavor of the man's personality. I include some small anecdotes because every observed facet of a man of such stature has the value of at least a chip to fill the cracks between the larger mosaic pieces in his portrait.

When I was permitted to make my first visit he had just emerged from a long, serious illness and was protecting himself. I arrived at the relatively remote house in Headington Quarry by taxi from Oxford. Lewis met me at the door and said it was difficult to get cabs and that I had better instruct the driver to come for me in an hour. I did so.

We hit it off reasonably well. When the cab drew up again, Lewis looked surprised, remembered, and said,

"Well, what a pity. You must come again and next time we won't tell the driver to come back." Then he laughed and said, "But after all, we couldn't know whether we'd like each other or not, could we?"

In Lewis' company I felt like a child. I have never felt myself in the presence of such depth and breadth of humane learning. Yet in no conscious way did Lewis "come over me" with it, in the English slang. It was simply what he was; it emanated from him. Thus I was struck when his close friend and fellow don, Nevill Coghill, testified in one of a collection of reminiscent essays by his friends (**Light on C. S. Lewis**, edited by Jocelyn Gibb, 1965): ". . . he was at first formidable in appearance, rather as Dr. Johnson . . . was formidable. There were many echoes of Johnson in Lewis. Both were formidable in their learning and in the range of their conversation, both had the same delight in argument, and in spite of their regard for truth, would argue for victory."

Yet there was a homeliness and material simplicity about him, compounded one suspects of the absent-mindedness about external things accompanying an intense inner life, and of an attachment to used things. On both my visits he was wearing a smoking jacket of incredible tatteredness, clearly a garment so loved and long used that he was oblivious of its state. He kept packing and lighting his pipe, as in one of the well-known photos, creating small eruptions of smoke and ashes.

This aspect of him is seen also in an aside, happily retained in the BBC conversation, which was held in Lewis' rooms in Magdalene College, Cambridge. Kingsley Amis rose at one point and was looking around.

Lewis: [interrupting himself] Are you looking for an ashtray? Use the carpet.

Amis: I was looking for the Scotch, actually.

Lewis: Oh, yes, do, I beg your pardon. . . . [then resumed his interrupted thought].

Later.

Amis: More Scotch?

Lewis: Not for me, thank you, help yourself. [Liquid noises.]

Amis: I think all this ought to stay in, you know—all these remarks about drink.

Lewis: There's no reason why we shouldn't have a drink.

I have given space to these small things to evoke the warm, intensely individualized man who carried an enormous burden of learning and used it to write a number of learned books. But he was the man who also lay in bed at nights seeing clear, detailed pictures of strange land-scapes on other planets, who struck from those visions, fictions exciting, amusing, moving, and, in that quality that he found in the visions of George Macdonald, holy. There is holiness and awesomeness—and still room for laughter— in the great council at Meldilorn in **Out of the Silent Planet**, and in the triumphant investiture as monarchs of the unfallen Adam and Eve of **Perelandra**, and the Great Dance of the Oyeresu—of all the heavenly bodies. The don and the lay theologian both are submerged in the wonder shared with us by the storyteller, and thus the learning and theology are transmitted as neither don nor theologian alone could transmit them. Pay homage to that gift—it is of God. And with it, Lewis served God, and us, and surely many to come after us.

5

John Warwick Montgomery

The chronicles of narnia and the adolescent reader*

IN 1956, THE CARNEGIE MEDAL, AWARDED ANNUALLY
FOR THE BEST CHILDREN'S BOOK PUBLISHED IN THE
BRITISH EMPIRE, was bestowed by the Library Association on Professor Clive Staples Lewis for his volume entitled
The Last Battle. This book was the seventh and last of
a unified series of works on the mythical land of Narnia—
a series begun by Professor Lewis in 1950 with the **The**

---

* Originally published in **Religious Education**, LIV/5 (September-October, 1959), 418-28, and here
reprinted with minor revisions. Commented Randolph Crump Miller of Yale to the readership
of **Religious Education** at the time this essay first appeared in print: "The editor believes that
John W. Montgomery's article on C. S. Lewis' Narnia chronicles has a three-fold importance:
it introduces us to Lewis and his writings, it evaluates an important series of books, and it
faces squarely the use of fantasy and allegory in religious communication." At the time of writing,
Dr. Montgomery was Head Librarian of the Swift Library of Divinity and Philosophy and a
member of the Federated Theological Faculty of the University of Chicago.

Lion, the Witch and the Wardrobe, and continued, at yearly intervals, by **Prince Caspian** (1951), **The Voyage of the "Dawn Treader"** (1952, **The Silver Chair** (1953), **The Horse and His Boy** (1954), and **The Magician's Nephew** (1955). The dearth of high-quality modern publications suitable for adolescents, together with a general lack of acquaintance with the Narnian Chronicles in this country, provides sufficient justification for a detailed examination of these works. In this article an attempt will be made to study both the literary quality of the Chronicles and the religious values which can accrue to the adolescent who reads them. It is sincerely hoped that the magic as well as the remarkable character of these volumes will become evident to the perusers of this study.

THE AUTHOR OF THE CHRONICLES

If the axiomatic truth is conceded that a book reflects the personality of its author, then there is good reason at the outset of this paper to become familiar with the basic facts of C. S. Lewis' life. Lewis was born November 29, 1898, the son of a Belfast Solicitor. His education at Oxford was interrupted by military service during the First World War, but was completed with honors. From 1924 until 1954, he was associated with Oxford in a teaching capacity (Fellow and Tutor of Magdalen College, 1925-1954). In 1954, he became Professor of Medieval and Renaissance English at Cambridge, which position he held until a short time before his death on November 22, 1963, the day of President Kennedy's assassination. He was married in 1957 to Joy Davidman Goesham, an American poet and novelist, who died only three years later. His scholarly honors included a D.D. from St. Andrews, a D. ès Lettrès from Laval University (Quebec), and election as a Fellow of the Royal Society of Literature and Fellow of the British Academy. His most famous scholarly publication is **The Allegory of Love** (1936; reprinted with corrections, 1938), a study of the medieval courtly love tradition with special emphasis upon its allegorical manifestations in literature.

But it is not as a professor or even as a medieval scholar that C. S. Lewis has attained his chief renown; it is rather as an apologist for the Christian faith. In his spiritual autobiography (**Surprised by Joy**, 1955), he informs us that his desertion of the Church of Ireland as a youth, and his acceptance of an atheistic philosophy of life, were followed by a quest for lasting satisfaction, or "joy"—and that this search finally led him, via the writings of George Macdonald, to an adult acceptance of Christian doctrine and membership in the Church of Ireland.[1] One result of his spiritual pilgrimage was the production of some of the most penetrating theological works of our time, all of them characterized by high literary quality. The most familiar of his writings is undoubtedly **The Screwtape Letters** (1942), the supposed correspondence of a senior devil in hell who instructs a minor demon on earth in the fine art of temptation. Lewis' work entitled **Miracles** (1947) is one of the most trenchant refutations ever written of Hume's argument against the miraculous. His BBC broadcast talks were published as **The Case for Christianity** (1943) and **Christian Behaviour** (1943, and have been reissued under the collective title, **Mere Christianity**). Professor Lewis also produced a trilogy of adult science fiction novels (**Out of the Silent Planet**, 1938; **Perelandra**, 1943; **That Hideous Strength**, 1945) through which various facets of the Christian gospel are presented allegorically. Allegory was extensively used with the same end in view in his **The Pilgrim's Regress** (1933) and **The Great Divorce** (1946).

The works here mentioned, together with Dr. Lewis' numerous other writings, have led to such evaluations of the man and his literary labors as the following:

> Classical Christianity—with or without mysticism—is one of the strongest contenders in the desperate race to replace that discredited secularism now visibly going to pieces. Of all

---

1. Lewis acknowledged his debt to Macdonald by editing **George Macdonald: An Anthology** in 1946.

the writers advocating Classical Christianity, none combines versatility, literary skill, and psychological insight so richly as C. S. Lewis. He is peculiarly capable of reaching and influencing the people who will influence the masses day after tomorrow.[2]

> When . . . we turn away from reading that is largely vocational—lawyers from legal tomes, doctors from their specialties, clerics from eschatology, educators from standardized tests, scientists from their individual deities of precision—if we no longer read history and biography avidly and if we no longer keep up the pretense that poetry is part of the natural reading of men interested in literature, let us permit C. S. Lewis and others with like gifts to remind us that men still write using a style and discussing a subject matter that is clear and clean; that the modern novelist or dramatist, for example, who frequently disturbs the muddy bottom of the pool and then invites us either to drink of dirty water or to swim in it is not the only type of person from whom we may receive invitations to refresh ourselves.[3]

Experience shows, however, that neither scholarly ability, nor skill as a novelist for adults, nor even good intentions, is any guarantee of success in the field of children's literature. We therefore turn our attention to Professor Lewis' seven Narnian Chronicles themselves.

THE CHRONICLES AS LITERATURE

Plots and Characters. Aristotle, in his **Poetics**, correctly asserted that the two central elements in a dramatic production were its characters and its plot—the latter being of greater consequence than the former. Each of the Narnian

---

2. Chad Walsh, **C. S. Lewis: Apostle to the Skeptics** (New York, Macmillan, 1949), p. 171. The bibliography at the end of Walsh's book gives a complete description of Lewis' publications through 1949. David Daiches, one of my former professors at Cornell University and now a professor at Cambridge University, writes of Lewis: "Such religious revival as there has been in postwar Britain appears to have been confined to the better educated. Its symbol is not Billy Graham, the American evangelist whose carefully staged campaigns caused considerable temporary excitement in 1954 and 1955, but, say, C. S. Lewis, a literary scholar and critic of considerable brilliance and at the same time a highly sophisticated Christian apologist" (**The Present Age in British Literature** [Bloomington, Indiana University Press, 1958], p. 13).

3. George F. Cassell, **Clive Staples Lewis** (Chicago, Chicago Literary Club, 1950), pp. 25-26.

books will now be described in terms of these two essential characteristics.

The Lion, the Witch and the Wardrobe introduces the reader, via the adventures of four English children, to the magical realm of Narnia—which is not "another planet, you know; they're part of our world and you could get to them if you went far enough—but a really other world—another Nature—another universe—somewhere you would never reach even if you travelled through the space of this universe for ever and ever."[4] The four children are Peter (a courageous youth on the borderline of adulthood), Susan (his slightly younger sister, rather timid, more interested in becoming an adult than in enjoying her present age), Edmund (their younger brother, of mean dispostion at the outset), and Lucy (the youngest of the four, bright, cheerful, spiritually discerning). These Pevensie children were sent to the country mansion of one Professor Digory Kirke in order to be safe from the London air-raids of the Second World War. While exploring and playing Hide-and-Seek in the fascinating old house, the children—first Lucy and then the others—enter Narnia through an old Wardrobe. Narnian time is not like Earth time, so whenever the children return to our world, they discover that no time at all has passed here. The children find Narnia a land of perpetual winter (but without Christmas ever coming), because the country is under the control of a White Witch from the North, who turns into statues all those inhabitants of the country who would oppose her. Edmund, principally out of jealousy toward Peter, sides with the White Witch, and is eventually made thoroughly miserable through his allegiance to her. The Witch's desire is to capture the four children, in order to thwart an old prophecy which says that "When Adam's flesh and Adam's

4. Lewis, **The Magician's Nephew** (New York, Macmillan, 1955), pp. 18-19. The Narnian Chronicles can be most cheaply obtained in their British editions (write: The Children's Bookshop, 22 Broad Street, Oxford).

bone/Sits at Cair Paravel (Narnia's capital) in throne,/ The evil time will be over and done." The citizens of Narnia (Talking Beasts, Fawns, and like creatures) feel sure that the coming of the children heralds a new age—and that the Great Lion named Aslan will soon destroy the White Witch's power. This is just what happens: the forces of the Witch are conquered in battle; Aslan himself gives his life so that Edmund's treachery will not receive its rightful consequences at the hands of the Witch (but Aslan is then miraculously restored); those turned to stone by the Witch become normal again when Aslan breathes on them; spring comes to Narnia; and the children are crowned Kings and Queens of Narnia, with Peter as High King.

In **Prince Caspian**, the Pevensies return to Narnia. One year has passed according to our time, but several hundred years have gone by in Narnia. The children were in a railway station ready to enter on another school year when—suddenly—they found themselves in Narnia again. Cair Paravel is in ruins. The land has for many generations been under the rule of the Telmarines, who, like the children, are "sons of Adam and daughters of Eve," but who conquered Narnia by an invasion from a neighboring country. Under Telmarine rule, no Talking Beasts or other mythical creatures dare live in the open, and the present (usurper) King has told his nephew, Prince Caspian, that all the old legends are "all nonsense, for babies." Caspian runs away, however, and the inhabitants of "Old Narnia" rally around him and a War of Liberation takes place. Caspian's forces are sorely pressed, and he blows a magic horn which had been given to Susan during her previous adventure in Narnia, and which had been found by the old tutor of the Prince. It was the blowing of this horn that brought the Pevensies into Narnia again. By Aslan's guidance they are led to the place where Caspian's forces are encamped, and Caspian's Uncle is defeated. Aslan then gives the Telmarines the choice of remaining in Narnia under Caspian's rule or returning to our world (from which they, as pirates, had originally come—through "one of the chinks or chasms between that world and this"). Some of the Telmarines choose Narnia, but most of the older men refuse to live in a land they cannot rule, and return to the Earth. The Pevensies find that their time to leave Narnia has come; and Aslan tells Peter and Susan that they are "getting too old" to visit Narnia again.

The Voyage of the "Dawn Treader" chronicles Edmund and Lucy's last adventure in Narnia—an adventure in which they are accompanied by their cousin, Eustace Clarence Scrubb. Before his visit to Narnia, Eustace was not the most likable chap in the world.

> He didn't call his Father and Mother "Father" and "Mother," but Harold and Alberta. They were very up-to-date and advanced people. They were vegetarians, non-smokers and teetotallers and wore a special kind of underclothes. . . . Eustace Clarence liked animals, especially beetles, if they were dead and pinned on a card. He liked books if they were books of information and had pictures of grain elevators or of fat foreign children doing exercises in model schools. Eustace Clarence disliked his cousins the four Pevensies. . . . But he was quite glad when he heard that Edmund and Lucy were coming to stay. For deep down inside him he liked bossing and bullying; and . . . he knew that there are dozens of ways to give people a bad time if you are in your own home and they are only visitors.

While gazing at a sea picture in the Scrubb home, Edmund, Lucy, and Eustace find themselves actually drawn into it, and they join King Caspian on a sea expedition. A year of Earth time has passed since Edmund and Lucy's last visit, and three years of Narnian time have gone by. Caspian has set out from Narnia to find seven nobles whom his Uncle, many years before, had gotten rid of by sending to explore "the unknown Eastern Seas beyond the Lone Islands." In the King's service is the mouse-knight Reepicheep, whose valor and singleminded allegiance to Aslan surpasses that of any other character in the Narnian

Chronicles; Reepicheep does not wish merely to find the seven lords—he wants to find the country of Aslan himself, which is supposed to lie beyond the world's end. Numerous Odyssey-like adventures occur on this voyage, such as Eustace's transformation into a dragon because of his greed and his restoration by the personal intervention of Aslan after he becomes humble and realizes how selfish he has been. The seven lords never reached the East, it is discovered; one married, settled for security, and ceased his Eastern journey; two died because of the fascination treasure and wealth held for them; one became enmeshed in his own dream-life; and three, at the very "beginning of the end of the world," never quite reached Aslan's country because of spiritual presumption and lack of love. When Caspian's ship, "The Dawn Treader," reaches the borderline between the Narnian world and Aslan's land, only Reepicheep crosses over. Caspian himself cannot go with him because of the responsibilities he has as King and because he was unkind to the others near the end of the journey; and Edmund, Lucy, and a transformed Eustace must return to their own world.

In **The Silver Chair,** Eustace and a school friend, Jill Pole, find themselves in Narnia at the very end of Caspian's reign. Ten years before, the Queen had been killed by a poisonous serpent while she was on a holiday in the northern part of Narnia. Her son, Prince Rilian, sought the serpent to kill it, but instead met a beautiful woman in green and was not seen again. Now Aslan has called Eustace and his friend into Narnia to find the Prince, for Caspian is close to death and has no other heir. Aslan gives them specific instructions, and they discover that when these are not precisely followed difficulties result on every side. They are accompanied on their journey to the Wild Lands of the North by Puddleglum, a cross between a man and a frog, who though of humorously pessimistic temperament ("what with enemies, and mountains, and rivers to cross, and losing our way, and next to nothing to eat, and sore feet, we'll hardly notice the weather"), is a stalwart servant of Aslan. They discover that the snake and the green lady are one in the same, and that for ten years she has kept Rilian entranced in her underground kingdom of almost total darkness—on the promise that as soon as she has undermined Narnia, she will give him his own land to rule (jointly with her, of course). With the aid of Eustace and Jill, Rilian destroys the Silver Chair which has caused his enchantment, and kills the green lady (the Queen of Underland), just in time to prevent the conquest of Narnia.

The Horse and His Boy "stands apart from the main cycle."[5] During the reign of High King Peter we are taken south from Narnia into the land of Calormen, whose government is similar to that of a medieval, oriental despotism on Earth. There we meet Shasta, an orphan boy who has been brought up by a harsh fisherman. One day Shasta meets a Narnian Talking Horse who was stolen from Narnia as a foal, and the two determine to escape to Narnia—or at least to Archenland, a kingdom allied to Narnia and directly south of it. The Talking Horse (named "Breehy-hinny-brinny-hoohy-hah," or "Bree" for short!) is a little too vain and proud, and quite critical of others, but is a nominal believer in Aslan, for, as he says, "All Narnians swear by **him**." On their journey, they meet two other émigrés: Aravis, the daughter of a Calormen lord who wished to marry her to an unpleasant old noble, and her Narnian Talking Horse named Hwin. In the Calormen city of Tashbaan, Shasta unexpectedly meets visiting Prince Corin of Archenland (who is almost his double). The two become friends, and express the hope of meeting again if Shasta makes good his escape. Aravis meanwhile overhears the treacherous plot of Rabadash, son of the Calormen King (or "Tisroc"), to capture Archenland without official declaration of war. With Aslan's guidance, Shasta,

5. M. S. Crouch. "Chronicles of Narnia," **Junior Bookshelf**, XX (Nov., 1956), 249. Cf. Kathryn Lindskoog, **The Lion of Judah in Never-Never Land: God, Man & Nature in C. S. Lewis' Narnia Tales** (Grand Rapids, Mich.: Eerdmans, 1973).

Aravis, and the Horses reach Archenland in time to save the country; defiant Rabadash is temporarily turned into a donkey by Aslan; Bree discovers what a vital, personal relationship with Aslan can be like; and Shasta finds that he is the long-lost brother of Prince Corin, and the next heir to the Archenland throne.

The Magician's Nephew provides the cosmological setting for all the Chronicles. Here we encounter Professor Digory Kirke again—but this time as a boy, back when "Mr. Sherlock Holmes was still living in Baker Street." Digory and his nextdoor neighbor, Polly Plummer, discover that Digory's Uncle is a magician of the evil, but rather simpleminded, variety. Through his magic they enter "The Wood between the Worlds," a place of connection among the numerous "worlds" (of which ours is only one) in the universe. First they visit a dying world—one which was destroyed by a Queen who, when she saw that she could not rule that world, determined to ruin it by uttering a "Deplorable Word" that she had discovered. Digory's selfish curiosity results in the awakening of that evil Queen, and she follows the children back into our world for a brief time, and then (together with Digory's Uncle and a kind London cabby) into a third world—Narnia—at the time of its creation. Here they witness Aslan as he builds a world ("when you listened to his song you heard the things he was making up: when you looked round you, you saw them"). Because Digory, a son of Adam, has brought evil (in the person of the Queen—or, as she would later be called, the White Witch) into Aslan's new world, Aslan commissions him to travel to a wonderful Garden in the Western Wild and there to pick an apple from a tree of life. This apple is to be planted in Narnia so that Narnia will have protection against the Witch for many years. Digory accomplishes his mission, and Aslan gives him a similar apple to revive his dying mother at home. The cabby remained in Narnia as her first King. After giving the apple to his mother, Digory buried the core in his backyard, and in later years built a wardrobe out of the tree that grew up from it—the same wardrobe, of course, through which the Pevensies would first enter Narnia.

The Last Battle records the final events in the history of Narnia. Several generations have passed since the reign of Caspian. An evil ape persuades a simple donkey that he should wear a lion's skin and pretend to be Aslan—thereby insuring that the Narnians will follow every order that the ape, as "Aslan's" mediator, gives them. The ape then enters into a compact with Calormenes, and soon many of the Narnians are engaged in slave labor activities by sanction of the pseudo-Aslan. The present King of Narnia, Tirian by name, can hardly believe that the true Aslan would allow his people to fall into slavery, and calls for help out of the past. Eustace and Jill arrive, but they are unable to stop the conquest of Narnia by the Calormenes, for by now many Narnians have come to believe that Aslan and the cruel god of Calormen (called "Tash") are really one ("Tashlan"), and others have become so disillusioned that they believe in the existence of neither. In the final battle, the children and Tirian suddenly find themselves in a Stable on the battlefield—a Stable which had housed the pseudo-Aslan and for a time had actually contained Tash. But "the Stable seen from within and the Stable seen from without are two different places"; indeed, "its inside is bigger than its outside." Inside, they find the previous Kings and Queens of Narnia, and those from our world who had been in Narnia before—the Pevensies, Professor Kirke, etc.—and all of them have become wondrously youthful and yet truly mature. Susan, however, is not among them; she "is no longer a friend of Narnia . . . Whenever you've tried to get her to come and talk about Narnia or do anything about Narnia, she says 'What wonderful memories you have! Fancy your still thinking about all those funny games we used to play when we were children.' . . . I wish she **would** grow up. She wasted all her school time wanting to be the age she is now, and she'll waste all the rest of her life trying to stay that age.") The inside of the Stable is a beautiful land—more beautiful than any they have ever seen. Aslan is there, and he brings about the end of Narnia on the outside of the Stable. Through the Stable door come creatures without number—including all the old animal and mythical friends of past adventures. Each looks into Aslan's face as he passes the doorway, and some go to the left and disappear, while others go to the right into the beautiful countryside. Aslan bounds away to the right— to the West—and all the creatures on his right follow him "farther up and farther in." They discover that they are in a new Narnia—more "real" than the former one. As one creature puts it, "I have come home at last! This is my real country! I belong here. This is the land I have been looking for all my life, though I never knew it till now. The reason why we loved the old Narnia is that it sometimes looked a little like this." When they arrive at the Garden in the Western Wild, it is Reepicheep who welcomes them; and the Garden turns out to be yet another Narnia—"like an onion: except that as you go in and in, each circle is larger than the last." This Narnia is a spur "jutting out from the great mountains of Aslan," and **real** England is seen as one of the many other spurs. Across the mountains the Pevensies see their own mother and father, and even Professor Kirke's old House—for in the **real** countries "no good thing is destroyed." Aslan then tells them that (as they vaguely suspected) the friends of Narnia were precipitated into the Stable from a fatal railway accident. "Your father and mother and all of you are—as you used to call it in the Shadowlands—dead. The term is over: the holidays have begun. The dream is ended: this is the morning.'

"And as He spoke He no longer looked to them like a lion; but the things that began to happen after that were so great and beautiful that I cannot write them. And for us this is the end of all the stories, and we can most truly say that they all lived happily ever after. But for them it was only the beginning of the real story. All their life in this world and all their adventures in Narnia had only been the cover and the title page: now at last they were beginning Chapter One of the Great Story which no one on earth has read: which goes on forever: in which every chapter is better than the one before."

The Allegory. The brief biographical sketch of C. S. Lewis given at the beginning of this paper indicated his strong interest both in Christian apologetics and in allegory. As the reader has already recognized from the plot summaries just presented, the Narnian Chronicles contain powerful and deep Christian allegory woven into their very fiber. It is this allegorical thread, more than any other factor, which makes of the Chronicles "an integrated single conception."[6] The theme is that basic of all themes, Redemption through Christ. In **The Voyage of the "Dawn Treader"** Lucy reads a wonderful story in a Magician's Book, and then tries to remember it. " 'How can I have forgotten?,' " she asks. " 'It was about a cup and a sword and a tree and a green hill, I know that much. But I can't remember and what **shall** I do?' And she never could remember ; ever since that day what Lucy means by a good story is a story which reminds her of the forgotten story in the Magician's Book."[7] And, needless to say, this is also what Professor Lewis means by a good story—one which will remind the reader of the One who was nailed to a tree on his behalf, and who now guides the believer, expects great things of him through faith, and waits to receive him into his everlasting kingdom when his work on earth is done.

Aslan is the Divine Christ—God revealed to creatures

---

6. Frank M. Gardner, "The Carnegie Medal Award for 1956," **Library Association Record**, LIX; 4th series, XXIV (May, 1957), 168.

7. Lewis, **The Voyage of the "Dawn Treader"** (London, Bles [1952]), p. 144. Cf. Lewis, "On Stories," **Essays Presented to Charles Williams** (London, Oxford University Press, 1947), pp. 90-105.

in a form in which they can at least partially understand him and love him.[8] In **The Lion, the Witch and the Wardrobe**, Aslan is not ultimately defeated when the Witch (**i.e.,** the Devil) demands, on the basis of "deep magic from the dawn of time" (**i.e.,** God's justice) that Edmund must pay with his life for his volitional allegiance to her. Aslan dies in Edmund's stead, and is resurrected through "deeper magic from **before** the dawn of time" (**i.e.,** God's love). In **Prince Caspian**, Narnia is redeemed from a different evil—from human beings who would force themselves upon and assert control over those whom Christ has put under his own authority and under the authority of the ministers (the Kings of Narnia) whom **he** has chosen. **The Voyage of the "Dawn Treader"** indicates the perils which a man encounters in seeking Christ's kingdom; Reepicheep is a glorious example of the person who "seeks first the Kingdom of God and His righteousness." **The Silver Chair** gives further insight into the strategy of the Demonic, which would plunge us into a world of spiritual darkness by pretending to give us the things to which God has **already** entitled us by His grace.[9] In **The Horse and His Boy** we see Christ's guiding hand over a person's life; at one point Aslan says to Shasta: "I was the lion who forced you to join with Aravis. I was the cat who comforted you among the houses of the dead. I was the lion who drove the jackals from you while you slept . . . , and I was the lion you do not remember who pushed the boat in which you lay, a child near death, so that it came to shore where a man sat, wakeful at midnight, to receive you."[10] **The Magician's Nephew** draws back the

---

8. Aslan is not simply "God," as Crouch asserts (**op. cit.,** p. 252), for he is referred to on several occasions as "the son of the Emperor over Sea" (e.g. in **The Voyage of the "Dawn Treader,"** p. 104).

9. Cf. Satan's appeal to Jesus in the wilderness: "The devil, taking him up into an high mountain, shewed unto him all the kingdoms of the world in a moment of time. And the devil said unto him, All this power will I give thee, and the glory of them: for that is delivered unto me; and to whomsoever I will I give it. If thou therefore wilt worship me, all shall be thine" (Luke 4:5-7).

10. Lewis, **The Horse and His Boy** (London, Bles, 1954), p. 147.

curtain on Creation,[11] and on the entrance of sin into a world through pride and presumption; and it shows us how easily a world can be destroyed through the ravages of such sin. In referring to the dying world which she visited, Polly asks, " 'But we're not quite as bad as that world, are we, Aslan?' 'Not yet, Daughter of Eve,' he said. 'Not yet. But you are growing more like it. It is not certain that some wicked one of your race will not find out a secret as evil as the Deplorable Word and use it to destroy all living things.' "[12] A timely warning in our age of atomic weapons! In **The Last Battle** the Biblical story of the end of human history is graphically portrayed: the Antichrist, the battle of Armegeddon, death (represented by the Stable which is larger on the inside than on the outside), the General Resurrection, and the consummation of the Plan of Redemption in a New Heaven and a New Earth.

And Narnia—what does Narnia itself symbolize? Narnia is a world, a state of mind, in which spiritual issues assume clarity, reality, and a place of paramount importance. The Pevensies are forbidden to return to Narnia when they reach adulthood not because Narnia is a mythical land only for children (as in the case in **Peter Pan**), but because they were brought to Narnia originally to learn the most basic lesson in life: that of seeking **first** God's Kingdom. Once learned, this lesson is to be applied in their own world. When the "Dawn Treader" had reached "the very end of the (Narnian) world,"

> between them and the foot of the sky there was something so white on the green grass that even with their eagles' eyes they could hardly look at it. They came on and saw that it was a Lamb.

---

11. Dr. Lewis is theologically correct in viewing Aslan (Christ) as Creator. According to John 1, "the word" (Christ) "was God. The same was in the beginning with God. All things were made by him; and without him was not any thing made that was made" (vs. 1-3).

12. **The Magician's Nephew**, pp. 159-60.

"Come and have breakfast," said the Lamb in its sweet milky voice.

Then they noticed for the first time that there was a fire lit on the grass and fish roasting on it.[13] They sat down and ate the fish, hungry now for the first time for many days. And it was the most delicious food they had ever tasted.

"Please, Lamb," said Lucy, "is this the way to Aslan's country?"

"Not for you," said the Lamb. "For you the door into Aslan's country is from your own world."

"What!" said Edmund. "Is there a way into Aslan's country from our world too?"

"There is a way into my country from all the worlds," said the Lamb; but as he spoke his snowy white flushed into tawny gold and his size changed and he was Aslan himself, towering above them and scattering light from his mane.

"Oh, Aslan," said Lucy. "Will you tell us how to get into your country from our world?"

"I shall be telling you all the time," said Aslan. "But I will not tell you how long or short the way will be; only that it lies across a river [i.e., the river of Death]. But do not fear that, for I am the great Bridge Builder. And now come; I will open the door in the sky and send you to your own land."

"Please, Aslan," said Lucy. "Before we do, will you tell us when we can come back to Narnia again? Please. And Oh, do, do, do make it soon."

"Dearest," said Aslan very gently, " you and your brother will never come back to Narnia."

"Oh, **Aslan**! !" said Edmund and Lucy both together in despairing voices.

"You are too old, children," said Aslan, "and you must begin to come close to your own world now."

---

13. Cf. Christ's post-Resurrection appearance to his disciples as recorded in John 21.

"It isn't Narnia, you know," sobbed Lucy. "It's **you**. We shan't meet **you** there. And how can we live, never meeting you?"

"But you shall meet me, dear one," said Aslan.

"Are—are you there too, Sir?" said Edmund.

"I am," said Aslan. "But there I have another name. You must learn to know me by that name. This was the very reason why you were brought to Narnia, that by knowing me here for a little, you may know me better there."

THE CHRONICLES AND THE ADOLESCENT[14]

Appeal. In determining the appropriateness of a book for a given age-group, two fundamental questions must be answered: Will the book appeal to readers of that age? and Does the book have definite value for readers of that age? We begin with the first of these questions, since, as Paul Hazard has pointed out in his **Books, Children, and Men,** adults have frequently done great harm to children by foisting upon them so-called "good" books which in reality have had little appeal for the children themselves.

The Chronicles of Narnia fall into that class of literature known as the "modern imaginative story" or "literary fairy tale," of which the most distinguished exemplar is undoubtedly **Alice in Wonderland**. The critics, in fact, have not been slow to class Professor Lewis' books with the latter. **The Manchester Guardian** wrote of **The Voyage of the "Dawn Treader,"** "C. S. Lewis keeps up his power to enter other worlds in the same dream-like and certain way as Hans Andersen or Lewis Carroll"; and **Books of Today** stated

---

14. In Professor Lewis' **Studies in Words** (Cambridge, Eng., Cambridge University Press, 1960), he speaks of "the downward path which leads to the graveyard of murdered words. First they are purely descriptive; **adolescent** tells us a man's age, **villain**, his status. Then they are specifically pejorative; **adolescent** tells us that a man's work displays 'mawkishness and all the thousand bitters' confessed by Keats, and **villain** tells that a man has a churl's mind and manners. Then they become **mere** pejoratives, useless synonyms for **bad**, as **villain** did and as **adolescent** may do if we aren't careful. Finally they become terms of abuse and cease to be language in the full sense at all." Needless to say, in the present essay we employ the term **adolescent** in its "purely descriptive" sense.

in its review of **The Lion, the Witch and the Wardrobe**, "This fairy tale is as good as any children's book written in the last twenty years and not unworthy to share a shelf with **Alice in Wonderland.**"

The problem, of course, is to discover at what age such imaginative stories exercise their appeal to readers. It is true that "the reading of fantasy really knows no age limits";[15] and it is also true that "some children heartily dislike fantasy."[16] But the question still remains: For those who like fantasy, at what age do books of the **Alice in Wonderland** variety have the deepest and most comprehensive appeal? Arbuthnot's decision with regard to **Alice** seems directly applicable to the Narnian Chronicles:

> When college students are asked what books they remember enjoying as children there is more disagreement over **Alice** than over any other book. Some disliked it heartily or were bored by it; some say **Alice** was one of their favorite books, not as children but at the high-school age. This is perhaps where it really belongs. Most of those who liked **Alice** as children, ten or under had heard it aloud by adults who enjoyed it.[17]

The greatest pleasure will undoubtedly be derived from the Narnian Chronicles when they can be appreciated both on the fantasy-adventure and on the allegorical level.[18] Until one reaches early adolescence, the allegory will almost certainly escape him; but if he waits until adulthood to read the tales, the adventure element may not exercise the breathless hold on him which it could at a younger

---

15. Josette Frank, **Your Child's Reading Today** (Garden City, Doubleday, 1954), p. 127. Cf. Lillian H. Smith, **The Unreluctant Years** (Chicago, American Library Association, 1953), chap. 10 ("Fantasy"), pp. 149-62.

16. May Hill Arbuthnot, **Children and Books** (Chicago, Scott, Foresman, 1947), p. 292.

17. **Ibid.**

18. The following statement by Gardner concerning the Narnian Chronicles is, in my opinion, woefully inadequate: "There is the same underlying theme of Christian mysticism as there is in Dr. Lewis' 'Perelandra' trilogy of adult novels, but that need not trouble the young reader. To him or her these are stories of an almost real but marvellous world, visited from time to time by young human beings, who have to prove their honour and worthiness to be in Narnia [!]" (**loc. cit.**).

age. In discussing "literature for young adolescents" (ages 13-14, grades 7-8), Bess Porter Adams includes in the constellation of reading interests eight items, of which five ("from atoms to planets," "pleasure with animals," "historical and adventure stories," "legendary hero tales," "books for laughter") are directly applicable to the Narnian Chronicles;[19] and she asserts: "Active as the adolescent is, he still finds time for day dreams. . . . Books may help satisfy the longings which lead to day-dreaming. The best of the adventure and imaginative stories stimulate and satisfy the reader's desire for romantic adventure while leaving him eager for personal action."[20] If this is granted, then there should be little doubt concerning the appeal of the Narnia books for the sensitive, imaginative young adolescent of junior high school age.

Value. But by no means all of the printed material which appeals to the adolescent is worth the time required to read it. In the discussion which followed his talk on children's literature at the Bournemouth Conference of the Library Association, Professor Lewis was questioned on the practical value of his fantasy tales; his answer is very illuminating.

> Mr. L. M. Bickerton (Worthing) considered that Dr. Lewis's paper had raised points that we as librarians must consider—our policy had been to provide more and more of the practical type of book written by authors like Ransome and De Selincourt that taught children how to handle boats, etc., but he wondered what practical use fantasy, such as Dr. Lewis advocated, could have for the child. Dr. Lewis agreed that practical things were first class, but that although fantasy might not help a boy to build a boat, it would help him immensely should he ever find himself on a sinking boat.[21]

---

19. Bess Porter Adams, **About Books and Children; Historical Survey of Children's Literature** (New York, Holt, 1953), chap. 9, pp. 235-57.

20. **Ibid.**, p. 256. Note in this connection the excellent essay by Padraic Colum entitled "Imagination and Children's Literature" and included in Phyllis Fenner, **The Proof of the Pudding: What Children Read** (New York, John Day, 1957), pp. 222-25.

21. Lewis, "On Three Ways of Writing for Children," **Library Association. Proceedings, Papers and Summaries of Discussions at the Bournemouth Conference 29th April to 2nd May 1952** (London, Library Association, 1952), p. 28 ("Discussion").

Here the basic issue is raised as to the value of the Narnian Chronicles: Does the child face significant problems of a deeper nature than material ones—problems which the Narnia books can aid in solving? Professor Lewis says Yes, and refers to such a basic religio-philosophical problem as death.

Robert J. Havighurst confirms Dr. Lewis' judgment when he presents as one of ten specific "developmental tasks" of adolescence the problem of "acquiring a set of values and an ethical system as a guide to behavior,"[22] and states that "the crowning accomplishment of adolescence is the achieving of a mature set of values and a set of ethical controls that characterize a good man and a good citizen."[23] As the Christian Church has recognized through its age-old rite of Confirmation (normally entered upon during early adolescence), the adolescent years are crucial for decision-making in the matter of a personal **Weltanschauung** or world-view.[24] If this is the case, we are led to ask: Can the Narnian Chronicles in fact aid in providing the adolescent with a meaningful life-orientation?

In his lecture "On Three Ways of Writing for Children," Professor Lewis says, "The two theories [of the fairy tale] which are most often in my mind are those of Tolkien and of Jung," and expresses the opinion that Tolkien's essay "is perhaps the most important contribution to the subject that anyone has yet made."[25] Jung's view (widely accepted both among psychoanalysts and among folklore scholars today) is that the fairy tale presents concepts and images which correspond to the basic universal symbols (or "Arche-

---

22. Robert J. Havighurst, **Developmental Tasks and Education**, 2d ed. (New York, Longmans, Green, 1952), pp. 62-71. Havighurst gives empirical data in support of this adolescent task in his **Human Development and Education** (New York, Longmans, Green, 1953), pp. 311-17.

23. **Ibid.,** p. 142.

24. Note that Amelia H. Munson astutely includes as one of five "dominant characteristics" of adolescence "audacity of belief" (**An Ample Field**, [Chicago, American Library Association, 1950], p. 8).

25. Lewis, "On Three Ways of Writing for Children," p. 24.

types") in man's unconscious mind.[26] Lewis agrees with this, but feels that Jung does not go far enough. "The mystery of primordial images is deeper, their origin more remote, their cave more hid, their fountain less accessible than those suspect who have yet dug deepest, sounded with the longest cord, or journeyed farthest in the wilderness."[27] J. R. R. Tolkien, Dr. Lewis believes, has succeeded in explaining the central significance of the fairy tale and its importance for life-orientation. Tolkien summarizes his position as follows:

> The Gospels contain . . . a story of a larger kind which embraces all the essence of fairy-stories. They contain many marvels—peculiarly artistic, beautiful, and moving; "mythical" in their perfect, self-contained significance; and at the same time powerfully symbolic and allegorical; and among the marvels is the greatest and most complete conceivable eucatastrophe.[28] The Birth of Christ is the eucatastrophe of Man's history. The Resurrection is the eucatastrophe of the story of the Incarnation. This story begins and ends in joy. It has pre-eminently the "inner consistency of reality." There is no tale ever told that men would rather find was true, and none which so many sceptical men have accepted as true on its own merits. For the Art of it has the supremely convincing tone of Primary Art, that is, of Creation. To reject it leads either to sadness or to wrath.
>
> It is not difficult to imagine the peculiar excitement and joy that one would feel, if any specially beautiful fairy-story were found to be "primarily" true, its narrative to be history, without thereby necessarily losing the mythical or allegorical significance that it had possessed. . . . The joy would have

---

26. See, e.g., C. G. Jung and K. Kerényi, **Einführung in das Wesen der Mythologie**, 4th ed. (Zurich, Rhein-Verlag, 1951).

27. Lewis, "Psycho-analysis and Literary Criticism," **Essays and Studies by Members of the English Association**, XXVII (1941), 21. Cf. Chad Walsh's penetrating observation: "The twentieth century is overwhelmingly psychological in its way of thinking and feeling—at least this is true of Western Europe and the United States. Lewis, perhaps deliberately, set himself in opposition. He decided, consciously or intuitively, that God's total creation is considerably more interesting and important than the turgid and elusive depths of the psyche, and that he would look outward rather than inward" ("C. S. Lewis: The Man and the Mystery," in **Shadows of Imagination**, ed. Mark R. Hillegas [Carbondale: Southern Illinois University Press, 1969], pp. 9-10).

28. Tolkien inserts a sentence at this point in the slightly revised version of the essay which appears in **Tree and Leaf** (London, Unwin Books, 1964), p. 62.

exactly the same quality, if not the same degree, as the joy which the "turn" in a fairy-story gives: such has the very taste of primary truth. (Otherwise its name would not be joy. [29]) It looks forward (or backward: the direction in this regard is unimportant) to the Great Eucatastrophe. The Christian joy, the **Gloria**, is of the same kind; but it is pre-eminently (infinitely, if our capacity were not finite) high and joyous. Because this story is supreme; and it is true. Art has been verified. God is the Lord, of angels, and of men— and of elves. Legend and History have met and fused. [30]

To Tolkien and to Lewis, tales such as the Narnian Chronicles can, by their very nature, serve as pointers to the great theme of Christian Redemption. Moreover, they will establish in the hearts of the sensitive reader an appreciation of, and a longing for, the Christian Story. If one believes that ethics cannot survive without proper inner motivation; that religion provides the only really effective ethical impetus which men have ever experienced; that Jesus made no mistake when he said, "I am the Way, the Truth, and the Life: no man cometh unto the Father, but by me" [31] (**i.e.,** that Aslan and Tash can never be fused into a Tashlan); and that adolescents in our culture need personal fellowship with the Lord Jesus more than they need anything else;—if we believe these things, then we shall unquestionably find the Chronicles of Narnia of lasting value to the adolescents whom we seek to win for Christ.

29. Cf. the title of C. S. Lewis' autobiography, referred to above: **Surprised by Joy**.
30. J. R. R. Tolkien, "On Fairy-Stories," **Essays Presented to Charles Williams**, pp. 83-84.
31. John 14:6.

6

Clyde S. Kilby

MYTHIC AND CHRISTIAN ELEMENTS IN TOLKIEN

MYTH NEEDS TO BE SEEN WITHIN A CERTAIN CONTEXT IF IT IS NOT TO APPEAR, to a modern audience at least, as negligible or silly. I want first to describe that context.

The two most basic characteristics of man, beyond his mere physical needs, is to know and to worship. The great Swiss psychologist Carl Gustav Jung thought that the urge toward knowing is so powerful that it brought about his birth and consciousness. "Meaninglessness," he said, "inhibits fullness of life and is therefore equivalent to illness."

Our present one-dimensional age is convinced that the main avenue to knowing is the making of statements. Yet all statements, indeed all systems, in becoming statements and systems, become self-destructive. One is at sixes and sevens to translate a language of one hundred thousand words into a language of one thousand words. This is man's predicament. What man is, what he feels himself to be, makes a wasteland of language. Yet because of man's insatiable desire to know he requires some sort of verbal actualization. He is like the old woman who said, "How do I know what I think until I hear what I say." Yet man's saying, i.e., his systemizing, is always inadequate. The more he defines, the more he abstracts, the farther a satisfying reality seems to fly. A young professor of philosophy said to me, "I feel I must write my own philosophy, yet by the end of the twenty years required to do the job, it will be so insufficient as to make the whole task foolish."

We intellectualize in order to know but, paradoxically, intellectualization destroys its object. The harder we grasp at the thing, the more its reality moves away, like the water and the fruit of Tantalus.

So what is to be done? Man finds in himself a third characteristic called imagination by which he can transcend statements and systems. By some magic imagination is able to disengage our habitual discursive and system-making habit and send us on a journey toward gestures, pictures, images, rhythms, metaphor, symbol, and, at the peak of all, myth. Jung speaks of "the slender hints of the knowable" and the need to discover mythic means of bringing these hints together. Systemizing drives essentiality away, but successful creativity attracts it. While the basic requirement of systemizing is abstracting, myth is concerned with wholes. Myth is necessary because reality is so much larger than rationality. Not that myth is irrational but that it accommodates the rational while rising above it.

Systemizing flattens, but myth rounds out. Systemizing

drains away color and life, but myth restores them. Myth
is necessary because of what man is, for he is less **homo
sapiens** than **sub specie aeternitatis**. The Roman poet Ovid
said that man was formed in the image of the gods and,
unlike animals, was given "a lofty countenance and ordered. . . . to contemplate the sky and to raise his erected
face to the stars." The finest explanation of myth is a remark
of long ago that man shall not live by bread alone. The
truth is that man is less fact than he is myth. Owen Barfield
thinks that man did not make myth but that myth made
man. Shortly before His crucifixion, Jesus told His disciples
that He was going away to prepare a place for them and
added, "whither I go ye know, and the way ye know."
The rationalist Thomas promptly retorted, "Lord, we know
not whither thou goest; and how can we know the way?"
Thomas, trying very hard to know the truth, wanted the
greatest Reality of all to be pinned down to here and there
on a flat map. The answer of Jesus was, "**I** am the way."
And a great living whole is always the answer of essentiality.
The Green Lady in Lewis' **Perelandra** learned what was
for her an astonishing truth from Ransom. "The world
is so much larger than I thought," she said. "I thought
we went along paths—but it seems there are no paths.
The going itself is the path." I think the rebelling students
at Harvard, at least some of them, realized something of
this essentiality when they posted among other signs on
campus one calling for more poetry in classroom lectures.

All statements, including the ones I am now making,
are unsatisfying because man is fundamentally mythic. His
real health depends upon his knowing and living his metaphysical totality. In myth man discovers and affirms not
his disparate nature but his mythic, his archetypal and
cosmic nature.

To define myth, as to define any other ultimate, is in
part at least to destroy it. Myth is as indefinable as man,
life, reality. To search for definitions is less to define than

to discover the paucity of words. It has been said that
the only good definition of poetry is a poetic definition.
So with myth. Myth is a way of going out into metaphysical
space and looking back and observing those mountains,
those rivers, those great blocks of land that only then can
be seen. A myth is a cosmic pattern which permeates man
by some osmotic design. Myth is one of the few means
by which to understand and possess the blue flower,
Sehnsucht, infinitude.

A blade of grass really seen, anything really seen,
suggests the transcendental nature of myth. Myth is the
dull name of a way of seeing, a way of knowing in depth,
a way of experiencing—a way that in being disinterested
contains the freedom of unending and vital interest. Mythic
insight tells us that plants and animals have "all the rights
and privileges thereunto appertaining." It will cause an
inevitable distinction between "thou" and "it." Lewis points
out that enchanted trees give all ordinary trees a measure
of enchantment. Myth is vision.

Jung makes much of consciousness. It has been pointed
out that consciousness and conscience are from the same
root and coincident in time. In man there is the exercise
of consciousness toward knowing and the exercise of conscience toward worship. Myth is, in Mircea Eliade's phrase,
"the nostalgia for eternity." Man's concept of the absolute,
he adds, "can never be uprooted: it can only be debased."
He points out, for instance, that sex was originally "a ritual
with transcendent meaning at every point." Those who
indulge in promiscuous sex perhaps know best the sordidness
of its unritual and animal uses. Our world presently is
dispossessed of hierarchy.

Myth is like the green-belt of the world without which,
as the great British historian George Macaulay Trevelyan
has said, man is brutish. Myth is a lane down which we
walk in order to repossess our soul, our essentiality. Myth,

said Charles Williams, consists of "patterns of the Logos in the depth of the sun." Coleridge said that symbol, myth's twin, is marked by "the translucence of the eternal through and in the temporal." Myth is ageless. Yet it may be experienced in some everyday act or thought suddenly alive with universal meaning. A friend asked William Blake, "When the sun rises, do you not see a round disk of fire something like a guinea?" to which he replied, "Oh no, I see an immeasurable company of the heavenly host crying, 'Holy, Holy is the Lord God Almighty.' " Jean Cocteau said that poetry is "a machine that manufactures love." Myth also manufactures love and truth and essentiality, or rather reveals them.

A perfect good, as well as a perfect anything else, is mythlike. The call of conscience toward perfect goodness is a mythic call lying beyond the best possible set of rules and regulations. Systematic philosophy and systematic theology are no more than statemental pointers, dry bran, beside the reality toward which they point. A common pursuit of many literary scholars in recent years has been the search for Christ-images. Tiresome as this study becomes when pressed too far, the fact remains that the images are there. They are there because, as St. Paul said, it is in God that man lives and moves and has his being. Those images are in civilized and uncivilized because the true Light lights every man coming into the world. The atheist Shelley noted that the ancient Prometheus hanging in infinite pain for doing good to man is strikingly like Jesus Christ on the cross. C. S. Lewis began a letter concerning **Till We Have Faces** by saying, "An author doesn't necessarily understand the meaning of his own story better than anyone else." That would be an almost insane remark except that **Till We Have Faces** is a myth, and in good myth an author puts not simply what he knows but what seems to have come from another world. Myth, Lewis felt, "does not essentially exist in words at all." For Tolkien man is a sub-creator,

the refracted Light
through whom is splintered from a single White
to many hues, and endlessly combined
in living shapes that move from mind to mind.[1]

And Tolkien goes on to say with much emphasis that man makes, that is, creates, by the same divine law by which he himself is made.

Now having endeavored to characterize myth, I wish to illustrate, if I can, the leading mythic element—that is, the religious—of **The Lord of the Rings**. I say the leading mythic element because there is no time now to cover all such elements. And secondly I wish to go further and endeavor to show that **The Lord of the Rings** has not simply a religious but also a clearly Christian meaning.

I am aware that such intentions are at once up against the stone wall of Professor Tolkien's denial that the story has any direct or allegorical implications. The story, says he, is "not 'about' anything but itself" and certainly "has **no** allegorical intentions, general, particular or topical, moral, religious or political." He declares in fact that he has a "cordial dislike" of allegory, and he says he began **The Lord of the Rings** just to amuse himself. To him it is "largely an essay in 'linguistic aesthetic,'" in which the story was made "to provide a world for the languages rather than the reverse."[2] Since hardly a page of this story can be read without clear and often momentous moral overtones, one seems to have little choice but to declare either that the author is really pulling one's leg or else to say with Edmund Wilson, a sworn foe of the story, that any pretentions to serious meaning in it is "all on the part of Dr. Tolkien's infatuated admirers."[3]

1. J. R. R. Tolkien, **Tree and Leaf** (London: Unwin Books, 1964), p. 49.
2. "Tolkien on Tolkien," **Diplomat**, October, 1966, p. 39.
3. Edmund Wilson, "Oo, Those Awful Orcs," **The Nation**, April 14, 1956, p. 312.

In view of this seeming inpasse between my stated subject and Professor Tolkien's objections to such a subject, I should like for awhile simply to overleap his objections and later return to them.

For what I believe to be the most comprehensive account of myth I turn to Mircea Eliade's **Cosmos and History**. Eliade identifies as the leading characteristic of myth "a revolt against concrete, historical time" and a "nostalgia for a periodical return to the mythical time of the beginning of things, to the 'Great Time.' " Archaic or mythic man takes the long view and endeavors, by what Eliade calls "paradigmatic gestures" to live not in ordinary time but recapture the golden time. Man remembers somehow a period of such beauty, glory, elemental purity, utter fresh-ness and Edenic joy that "neither the objects of the external world nor human acts, properly speaking, have any autonomous intrinsic value. Objects or acts acquire a value, and in so doing become real, because they participate, after one fashion or another, in a reality that transcends them." Hence ordinary time—the sort identified with newspapers and the passing scene—has little interest. The true reality is that of a Golden Age which has long since disappeared, an age toward which the deepest yearning of the heart is turned, a true and trustworthy Reality which strongly contrasts with the relative triviality of current events, the "getting and spending" of life. Mythic man is concerned with being rather than with mere living.

All the more stirring portions of **The Lord of the Rings** seem to be quite a perfect illustration of Eliade's characteri-zation of myth. To make a simple hierarchical arrangement of peoples in Tolkien's story is itself to suggest the trans-cendent and mythic quality. On the bottom rung are the orcs and the debased Gollum, creatures of the here-and-now who are filled with loathing for light and for anything originating in Lothlorien, such as lembas, the Westernessmade knives of Merry and Pippin, the very name "Elbereth," and the like. At a much higher level are the hobbits, who recall their intricate genealogical connections and the quiet joys of the Shire. Again, the dwarves recall Durin, their first-age ancestor and the ancient glories of Moria where

> Beneath the mountains music woke:
> The harpers harped, the minstrels sang,
> And at the gates the trumpets rang. (I, 330)[4]

As with the dwarves, the vision of men is a long one. Sam and Frodo noted its far reach when at Henneth Annun in the woods of Ithilien Faramir and his men before meals looked "towards Numenor that was, and beyond to Elven-home that is, and to that which is beyond Elvenhome and will ever be" (II, 284-85).

But it is the elves whose hearts are unceasingly aware of their ancient and transcendent past when "the secret fire was sent to burn at the heart of the world." King Theoden asked Gandalf about the "wizardry" by which the trees had destroyed Saruman's fortress. "It is not wizardry," said Gandalf, "but a power far older, a power that walked the earth, ere elf sang or hammer rang,

> Ere iron was found or tree was hewn,
> When young was mountain under moon;
> Ere ring was made, or wrought was woe,
> It walked the forests long ago." (II, 149, 174)

Treebeard informs Merry and Pippin that the early Elves were the Adam-namers (II, 86).

These allusions are mainly to the glory of early Middle-earth, but there are even more Edenic allusions to Valinor and the Blessed Realm. We are told that "all lore was in these latter days fallen from its fullness of old" (III,

---

4. All references to Tolkien's epic apply to the three-volume, hard-cover edition (London: Allen & Unwin; Boston: Houghton Mifflin, 1966).

136). Earendil's experience is an instance of reverence for the deep past. In the first age, Earendil, desperate for aid for his people against Morgoth, built a glorious rune-protected ship and sailed "beyond the days of mortal lands." Lost in starless waters, he was visited by Elwing who bound on him one of the three silmarils which had long before been created by Feanor (whose name means "Spirit of Fire") to hold the light of the golden and silver trees. With this light he retraced his way and finally came to Elvenhome, "the green and fair," where he was clothed in elven-white and sent inland through the Calacirian entrance to

> timeless halls
> Where shining fall the countless years,
> and endless reigns the Elder King. (1, 248)

There in the Blessed Realm he heard such sacred words and saw such visions that he could not again return to Middle-earth, whereupon the undefiled dwellers in Ilmarin built a majestic ship for him and Elbereth Gilthoniel, Queen of the Valar and maker of the stars, set the silmaril on that ship as an everlasting light and set him as a star to travel through the skies. Whenever the elves see that star they are poignantly reminded of a glory hardly of this world.

In Middle-earth, Rivendell and particularly Lothlorien are symbols of Eliade's "Paradise." "Time doesn't seem to pass here" (I, 243), said Bilbo of Rivendell, and Professor Tolkien told me that he could not reread his own account of Lothlorien without emotion. The elves are always reminded by Lothlorien, their paradisal land, of the true paradise of the Blessed Realm, and in turn the succor which Lothlorien gives to the members of the Fellowship, and even its natural enemy Gimli, creates a blessedness that is ever after to remain warm, elevating and enticing in their memory. Thus the recollection of sacred time which echoes in Lothlorien becomes a reecho in Gimli and the others. Galadriel's phial of light, taken from Earendil's star and redolent of a light existing even before that, and so utterly comforting and protective to Frodo and Sam as they move toward the dark terrors of Mordor, is perhaps the best symbol in **The Lord of the Rings** of Eliade's Great Time, for around the phial clings the whole glory of the Age of Gold when "heaven" was emptied of some of its angelic beings who voluntarily descended to Middle-earth for the establishment of a kingdom commensurate with a heavenly vision which had been shown them. That phial contained light created before the sun itself, a light first resident in Telperion and Nimloth, the two trees, white and golden, that belonged to a period of some sixty thousand years before and more properly are outside time altogether. Here is a thing which can be held in the hand that is essentially paradisal.

Eliade's "paradigmatic gesture" is illustrated by the quality and quantity of allusions to such elements as this phial of light, but far more so by the songs. There is a tendency to sing both in times of great joy and times of great stress. There is singing in Rivendell and Lothlorien and also in the horror of Moria and the farewell to Lothlorien and "the Lady that dies not." In the hell of Mordor the songs, yet not altogether the memories, disappear for Frodo and Sam, yet after Orodruin and rescue the songs begin again. The truth is that Tolkien's world is arched with timelessness and thickset with a glory, a timelessness and glory felt by each member of the Fellowship but particularly poignant for the elves. Lovers of the story feel as if it is a thing not so much to be read as to be sung. It is a story of the movement from eternity to time and therefore of sadness. It is a book of infinite losses, of cosmic diminution, of paradise lost, and yet not without its eucatastrophe and evangelium.

Some of the most poignant turns of the story are those in which certain elves must decide between sacred and profane

time, as in the case of Arwen Evenstar. The sad parting
of the Fellowship at the end of the story is made far sadder
by the farewell of Arwen Evenstar and her father after
Arwen, for love of Aragorn, had chosen profane time.
Arwen's general farewell was public, but her last meeting
with her father Elrond, who belonged to sacred time, was
private. "None saw her last meeting with Elrond her father,
for they went up into the hills and there spoke long together,
and bitter was their parting that should endure beyond
the ends of the world"(III, 256). Arwen's choice of profane
time repeated the long previous love choice of another elf
for a man, that is, of Melian the Maia who filled the silence
of Arda before the dawn with her voice. Thingol came
upon her dancing in Nan Elmoth, loved her so much that
they stood hand in hand for long years, and together they
became the rulers of the Grey Elves.

I must now leave this meagre illustration of **The Lord
of the Rings** as myth in Eliade's sense and pass along
to the main idea I wish to stress—that of the story as
essentially a Christian narrative.

One of the most obvious Christian intimations, as others
have pointed out, arises in the two worlds depicted—one
all but angelic, the other hellish. There is a Fellowship
of the good and upright and a parallel "fellowship" of the
evil. To be sure, the evil is a company fettered together
by its diabolical leader Sauron—whose name is strongly
suggestive of **saurian** or reptilian—but its members have
the effect of working as a body with relatively little inter-
necine struggle or opposition. We are told that Mordor
"draws all wicked things" to itself.

The most dominant symbol of these two worlds is the
contrast of darkness and light. Sauron is called the Black
Hand, Black Master, Black One, Black Shadow, Dark Lord,
Darkness, Dark Power, the Enemy, the Lord of the Black
Lands, etc. The Tower of Ecthelion standing high above

the topmost walls of Minas Tirith "shone out against the
sky, glimmering like a spike of pearl and silver, tall and
fair and shapely, and its pinnacle glittered as if it were
wrought of crystals; and white banners broke and fluttered
from the battlements" (III, 23). Sauron's tower, on the other
hand, rises "black, blacker and darker than the vast shades
amid which it stood" (III, 219). The white tree is the symbol
of the ancient Blessed Realm. White clothing is nearly
always a symbol of goodness in the wearer, while the black
robes of the Ringwraiths clearly identify their stealthy and
perpetual evil. At the Ford of Bruinen the black horses
of the Ringwraiths contrast with the transcendent whiteness
of Glorfindel's horse which carries Frodo to safety. The
same transcendency identifies Glorfindel himself who is,
we learn, one of the mighty of the Firstborn who had once
dwelt in the Blessed Land (I, 235). Hardly is there a more
dreadful picture in all of **The Lord of the Rings** than Shelob
coming out of her black hole under a cliff with her great
swollen body blotched with livid spots, her stinking belly,
and her knobbly, hairy legs and claws (II, 334). What could
save the diminutive hobbits from such an enemy? Not
strength or ingenuity but the remembrance that they carry
on their person the phial of light given them by Galadriel
in heavenly Lothlorien. When they thrust this phial before
the evil cluster of Shelob's eyes, it created a terror she
had never experienced before, "the dreadful infection of
light." Afterwards the hobbits recollected that it was light
from the Blessed Realm, a light to light them "in dark
places, when all other lights go out" (I, 393). The giver
was Galadriel, "the Lady that dies not," and who bore
about her a glory reminding one of the luminosity of Dante's
Beatrice or of his image of the Virgin.

The light of sun, moon and stars is hated by the orcs
and other evil characters but loved by the good ones. Gollum
looks up at the moon and blinks and says it is a "Nassty,
nassty shiver light" that spies on him. The orcs travel
at night because of their hatred of the sun, and Mordor

is represented as a place where dark clouds often hover near the ground. The utter darkness of Moria and of the Barrows has a potency like that of Hades, which Job described as "a land of darkness, as darkness itself . . . where the light is as darkness (Job 10:22). The good people in **The Lord of the Rings** love light. Completely alone and feeling totally forsaken inside Mordor, Sam slips away from the sleeping Frodo to reconnoitre and, happening to look beyond the dark and treacherous mountain above him, saw a white star twinkling. "The beauty of it smote his heart . . . and hope returned to him. For like a shaft, clear and cold, the thought pierced him that in the end the Shadow was only a small and passing thing: there was light and high beauty for ever beyond its reach" (III, 199). He returned to Frodo calm and hopeful and fell into an untroubled sleep. Earlier Sam, remembering the history of their phial of light, said to Frodo, "We're in the same tale still," a suggestion of their solemn connection with ancient and sacred history. **The Lord of the Rings** is a story in which fixed and eternal things accommodate themselves to all the principal actions.

In a doctoral dissertation at Columbia University, Mariann B. Russell concludes that Lewis, Williams and Tolkien all "shared a belief that the thrill of adventure could be related to the romantic experience which in its turn could be related to Christian theology." Dorothy K. Barber, in her dissertation at the University of Michigan, goes farther and insists that in Tolkien's story there is "a coherent and consistent significance which is largely Christian" and draws its special qualities from the Bible. She says explicitly, "The basis for **The Lord of the Rings** is the metaphor, God is light." If this is true, then the converse representation of evil as darkness is to be expected.

Again, the Quest itself has the earmarks of a Christian dedication. When Frodo at the beginning of the story learns from Gandalf something of the dangers, he says: "I am not

made for perilous quests. . . . Why was I chosen?" (I, 70, 71).
It is the same question asked by Ransom when faced
by the devil-possessed Unman in C. S. Lewis' **Perelandra.**
And the same answer is given to Frodo and Ransom. To
Frodo it was said, "You may be sure that it was not for
any merit that others do not possess: not for power or
wisdom, at any rate. But you have been chosen, and you
must therefore use such strength and heart and wits as
you have." Later at the Council of Elrond, Frodo, knowing
now from his experience at Weathertop the malignancy
of the Ringwraiths and learning the full magnitude of the
task before him, quietly and "as if some other will was
using his small voice," said, "I will take the Ring, though
I do not know the way" (I, 284).

That there is some superordinating power over Frodo
and his friends is often suggested. There is a force "beyond
any design" of Sauron, says Gandalf, as he explains the
history of the Ring to Frodo. Bilbo, he says, "was **meant**
to find the Ring," and therefore Frodo was also "**meant**
to have it" (I, 65). Elrond tells those present at the Council
that though they are seemingly there by chance, it is not
actually so. "It is so ordered that we, who sit here, and
none other, must now find counsel for the peril of the world"
(I, 255). A little later Aragorn tells Frodo pointedly that "it
has been ordained" that he should hold the Ring (I, 260).
Proud Boromir is a believer in strength and power
and finds it hard to understand Frodo's assurance that
they must not trust "in the strength and truth of men"
(I, 413-14). Like MacPhee in C. S. Lewis' **That Hideous
Strength**, Boromir thinks that in a time of great trouble
it is foolish to wait for supernatural guidance and help.
Though Tolkien feels that the Christian element in Lewis
is too explicit, one finds frequent parallels in which the
veil is hardly less transparent in Tolkien's story. In both
a sovereign Good is constantly and consistently operative.

I have already mentioned the search for Christ images

in modern literature. They are by no means infrequent in **The Lord of the Rings**. For instance, Gandalf's struggle with the fiery Balrog, a denizen of deepest and darkest underground, as both fall into a bottomless chasm, is strongly suggestive of Christ's descent into hell, and after Gandalf's resurrection—it is plainly called a resurrection—the Fellowship gazed on him with something of the same astonished joy that Mary Magdalene and others found at the tomb of Christ. Gandalf's hair, we are told, was "white as snow in the sunshine; and gleaming white was his robe; the eyes under his deep brows were bright, piercing as the rays of the sun; power was in his hand" (II, 98). Gimli the dwarf sank to his knees and shaded his eyes from Gandalf's brightness. Later we learn that Gandalf is "filled with light," his head is "now sacred" (II, 107), he is a healer, does not require armor in battle, etc. We learn also that a whole year would not be sufficient for him to tell of his struggle with the Balrog underneath the earth (II, 104). It is significant that Gandalf says he has "no lasting abode" (III, 365) in the earth, also that there has never been a day when he and other "wanderers" of the world have not guarded the Shire with watchful eyes.

I do not find it difficult to see as Christ symbols Frodo's commitment at Rivendell and most of his and Sam's journey after leaving their friends, and particularly the desperate journey through Mordor, the climax of that journey on Mount Doom, the sacrifice of life they expect to make, and the unexpected triumph and fruits of victory. Take as an instance Frodo's remark to Sam as they make the last struggle across the pits of Gorgoroth and up Orodruin and Frodo comes more and more under the burden of the Ring. He says to Sam, "No taste of food, no feel of water, no sound of wind, no memory of tree or grass or flower, no image of moon or star [note that now not even the stars can help] are left to me. I am naked in the dark, Sam, and there is no veil between me and the wheel of fire" (III, 215). Does this not suggest something of the desperation that at least **we** feel as we go through the events of the last day or so of Christ's life on earth? Frodo resists the protection of the One Ring, throws off his orc disguise, and goes straight forward to his destiny. It seems to me that Frodo's last momentary determination not to destroy the Ring has at least a little in it of Christ's cry from the Cross, "My God, why hast thou forsaken me?" A further hint of such a suggestion is the fact that in the darkness on top of Orodruin not even Galadriel's phial can throw much light (III, 222). At the last moment as Frodo and Gollum teeter on the edge of the precipice, Sam catches a visionary glimpse of them standing like personifications of Good and Evil, Gollum a creature "filled with a hideous lust and rage" and Frodo "a figure robed in white" holding at its breast a wheel of fire (III, 221). Good overcomes Evil, but the struggle ends in a cosmic climax.

Yet after the struggle comes the Triumph, and the reader is deeply stirred by the—to use Tolkien's own significant word—Eucatastrophe. Sam and Frodo totter down to an ashen hill at the foot of Orodruin and there fall side by side to await death. But then comes the "sent" eagles and the faithful servants are picked up and carried away from the stench and the rivers of fire, and the next thing they know is a soft bed underneath beechen boughs glimmering green and gold through the lovely woods of Ithilien. Sam thought it was a dream but then discovered beside him Gandalf, "robed in white, his beard now gleaming like pure snow in the twinkling of the leafy sunlight." They learn that "the King" awaits them. Sam asks, "Is everything sad going to come untrue?" and is told yes.

'A great Shadow has departed,' said Gandalf, and he laughed, and the sound was like music, or like water in a parched land; and as he listened the thought came to Sam that he had not heard laughter, the pure sound of merriment, for days upon days without count. It fell upon his ears like the echo of all the joys he had ever known. But he himself burst into tears. Then, as a sweet rain will pass down a wind of spring and the sun will shine out the clearer, his tears

ceased, and his laughter welled up, and laughing he sprang
from his bed.

'How do I feel?' he cried. 'Well, I don't know how to say
it. I feel, I feel'—he waved his arms in the air—'I feel like
spring after winter, and sun on the leaves; and like trumpets
and harps and all the songs I have ever heard!' (III, 230)

The apocalyptic overtones of such a scene can hardly be
avoided. But there is more.

The returning King they discover to have been their
dear companion all the way, Aragorn the wandering ranger
who has long guarded the world from dangers, who is
believed to have strange powers of sight and hearing, who
understands the languages of beasts and birds and in other
ways might symbolize the kingship and the omniscience,
omnipotence and loving omnipresence of Christ. Aragorn
has "taken back all his ancient realm. He will ride soon
to his crowning" (III, 230). When Frodo and Sam come
into his presence, he at first gently recalls to them how
they had originally disbelieved in him, but then he takes
them by the hand, "Frodo upon his right and Sam upon
his left" and leads them to his throne. There the two
"nobodies" hear the well-done first of the King himself
and then of all the people, and there is almost unspeakable
joy.

And all the host laughed and wept, and in the midst of
their merriment and tears the clear voice of the minstrel rose
like silver and gold, and all men were hushed. And he sang
to them, now in Elven-tongue, now in the speech of the West,
until their hearts, wounded with sweet words, overflowed, and
their joy was like swords, and they passed in thought out to
regions where pain and delight flow together and tears are
the very wine of blessedness. (II, 232)

The whole scene is evocative of the last pages of the Bible
and also suggests Saint Augustine's answer to a question
that deeply perturbed him in his relationship to God:

But what do I love, when I love Thee? not beauty of

bodies, nor the fair harmony of time, nor the brightness
of the light, so gladsome to our eyes, nor sweet melodies
of varied songs, nor the fragrant smell of flowers, and oint-
ments, and spices, not manna and honey, not limbs accept-
able to the embracements of flesh. None of these I love, when
I love my God; and yet I love a kind of light, and melody,
and fragrance, and meat, and embracement when I love
my God, the light, melody, fragrance, meat, embracement of
my inner man: where there shineth unto my soul what space
cannot contain, and there soundeth what time beareth not
away, and there smelleth what breathing disperseth not, and
there tasteth what eating diminisheth not, and there clingeth
what satiety divorceth not. This is it which I love when I
love my God.[5]

Since nothing less than the devilish enslavement of all
Middle-earth to incarnate evil has been at stake, and since
the meek and obedient have won the victory and inherited
that earth, we feel that a poignant, epic and indeed heavenly
joy is appropriate.

But at the same time there hangs heavily over **The
Lord of the Rings** the melancholy note of evil as an enduring
fact. All three ages have seen devastating evil. When **The
Silmarillion** is published it will be clear that Melkor, later
called Morgoth, is nothing less than one of the angelic spirits
who came into the world to make it after the pattern shown
in "heaven" and who like Satan revolted and in due course
enticed Sauron, another such angelic spirit, to become his
servant in evil. In the second age the great revolt took
place in Numenor and was engineered by Sauron, who had
been brought to that lovely land as a prisoner. Both the
cause and the result of the revolt are highly suggestive
of Biblical events. Sauron persuaded the Numenoreans
that if they ignored the ban of the Valar and made their
way over forbidden waters and once set foot on the shore
of Aman the Blessed, they would be like the Valar and
possess everlasting life.

---

5. Augustine, **Confessions**, trans. Edward B. Pusey (New York: Washington Square Press, 1962),
p. 177.

The crime of the Numenoreans is very similar to that in Lewis' **That Hideous Strength**: it is nothing short of the intention of turning men into gods. As a result of this revolt the island of Numenor was caused to sink into the sea. But, as with Noah, a few of the faithful are saved and make their way by ship from Numenor to Middle-earth and there establish themselves. Thus evil in **The Lord of the Rings** is cosmic and seemingly endless and will make forage of all good unless overcome by forces like those of the Fellowship and particularly by individuals committed as was Frodo. (The fact that the Fellowship consists of so varied a personnel as elves, dwarves, hobbits, and men is itself perhaps significant.)

Along with this continuing evil, however, comes always the possibility of redemption. The evil, in fact, clearly appears in people who were once good and therefore know the way back home. It is made completely clear that not even Morgoth and Sauron were evil in the beginning (I, 281). The tragedy of Saruman's great descent from membership in the White Council to a cackling lump of resentment and envy is sharp and strong in the story. But even in the moment of his lowest degradation when he makes an attempt upon Frodo's life, Frodo stops Sam from killing him. "He was great once," says Frodo, "of a noble kind that we should not dare to raise our hands against. He is fallen, and his cure is beyond us; but I would still spare him, in the hope that he may find it" (III, 299).

The Ringwraiths were once good men of Numenor who were enticed into Sauron's camp by a promise similar to that of Eden, i.e., the promise of knowledge (I, 255). In all these cases the compassion, I think, surpasses the norm of ordinary morality. It has the quality of mercy such as Portia calls "an attribute of God himself." When Frodo tells Gandalf that it was a pity Bilbo did not kill Gollum when he had the chance, Gandalf reprimands Frodo. "It was," says he, "Pity [note the capital] that stayed his hand.

Pity, and Mercy: not to strike without need" (I, 68).
Frodo finally learns this pity and practices it even after
Gollum has spit in his face.

Again the conception of evil as having no essential being
is remarkably suggested by the presentation of Sauron and
his immediate henchmen as wraiths. We are told once that
the horses the Ringwraiths ride are real but that the black
robes worn by the Ringwraiths "give shape to their nothing-
ness" (III, 103). I have mentioned that Frodo took on ever
so little the wraith-like quality by his use of the Ring at
Weathertop. The skulking Gollum, we are told, is simply
"the shadow of a living thing" (III, 221).

In the same connection we can mention the inability
of evil to create anything but only to mock. In the first
age it was believed that Morgoth captured some of the
elves newly come into the world and slowly bred them
into orcs in envy of the Eldar. This was regarded as one
of his vilest deeds. He also made trolls in mockery of the
Ents. Of the orcs, we are told, "The Shadow that bred
them can only mock, it cannot make: not real new things
of its own" (III, 190). It did not give life to the orcs, "it
only ruined them and twisted them." Philosophers and
theologians have often noted the inessentiality of evil.
C. S. Lewis says, "The Devil could **make** nothing but has
infected everything." [6]

I think also that the element of will in the Tolkien story
rises above that of simple Stoicism and takes on something at least of a Christian color. Frodo's heartfelt commitment to the cause does not save him and Sam from an
increasing need to command their wills as they move deeper
and deeper into enemy territory. Their whole way through
Mordor is that of dedicated hearts careless of their own
safety except as that safety pertains to the fulfilling of

---

6. **Letters of C. S. Lewis**, ed. with a Memoir by W. H. Lewis (London: Bles, 1966), p. 301.

their purpose. As they neared Mount Doom, the weight of the Ring and the steadily increasing desire of Frodo to use it as a means of escape became a battleground in his inner parts and forced him over and over to will against the easy way. One of the powers of the Ring is by destroying selfhood to bring the user into the dominion of Sauron, to turn him from a being into a wraith. One of the clear evidences of Frodo's increasing greatness of character is his steady will to resist incredible temptation in the face of growing physical weakness. Saint Augustine's doctrine of the effective will is well illustrated by Frodo.

Echoes and overtones of a theistic, Biblical world appear everywhere. Except for a reversal of the sexes, the marriage of elves and men suggests Genesis 6:4, where we are told that "the sons of God came into the daughters of men, and they bore children to them." The long lives of certain characters in **The Lord of the Rings** suggest the Biblical patriarchs. Elrond performs a miracle at the Ford of Bruinen by causing the waves of water to strike down the Ringwraiths who are upon Frodo (I, 236), and to further aid Frodo there appears a shining figure, Glorfindel, from "the other side," i.e., the Blessed Realm. There are prayers to "saints" like Elbereth Gilthoniel and Galadriel (I, 208; III, 195; etc.), and Aragorn calls on the name of Elendil in the thick of the fight with the Balrog (I, 345). The lembas can easily be taken as a symbol of the Eucharist. The body of Sauron perished in the collapse of Numenor and he returned to Middle-earth as an evil spirit to lead and control other evil spirits (III, 317), the Ringwraiths, suggesting the "principalities" and "powers" and "the rulers of the darkness of this world" of Ephesians 6:12.

One clear contrast between Frodo and Sauron is perhaps best understood from a Biblical viewpoint. Summing up the account of the people of faith, Hebrews 11:34 (Phillips paraphrase) says, "From being weaklings they became strong men and mighty warriors"—not an inept description of Frodo, just another hobbit who, like Sarah Smith of Golders Green in **The Great Divorce**, would hardly be noticed but who had greatness within. On the other hand, Sauron's empire, though powerful, has most of it trappings outward and therefore as subject to a total collapse as was the giant Goliath when struck by the smooth stone of the youthful David.

The eagles which rescue Frodo and Sam at Orodruin may be seen, I think, either as a rather feeble example of the **deus ex machina** or else as a Biblical symbol such as that of Exodus 19:4, where God said to Moses, "Have you seen what I did to the Egyptians, and how I bore you on eagles' wings and brought you to myself?" And I do not believe it is an accident that Tolkien in that moving account of the partings of the Fellowship has Arwen Even-star take "a white gem like a star" (III, 253) and hand it over to Frodo, the symbol of her rights to the Blessed Realm itself. This gem surely suggests Revelation 2:17: "To him that overcometh will I give . . . a white stone, and in the stone a new name written." That the rights of the stone eventuate is clear from that glorious passage in which Galadriel and Frodo's ship passes into the West, "until at last on a night of rain Frodo smelled a sweet fragrance on the air and heard the sound of singing that came over the water. And then it seemd to him that . . . the grey rain-curtain turned all to silver glass and was rolled back, and he beheld white shores and beyond them a far green country under a swift sunrise" (III, 310). The beatific has finally reached a little hobbit who insisted that he was not made for perilous quests but who nevertheless followed the Grail.

And so we might go on, but now it is necessary to return to Professor Tolkien's insistence that **The Lord of the Rings** has "**no** allegorical intentions, general, particular or topical, moral, religious or political." Let me say a few things that may help to clarify.

First, Professor Tolkien was himself a devout Christian. My summer's experience with him convinced me both of his wide Biblical interest and his deep convictions about sin and salvation through Christ. Once he showed me an unpublished paper by a British professor the idea of which was that **The Lord of the Rings** is misunderstood by critics because they failed to see that it is based on the manner of Christ's redemption of the world. To this Tolkien said, "Much of this is true enough—except, of course, the general impression given . . . that I had any such 'schema' in my conscious mind before or during writing." It was against this ticketed didacticism that Tolkien found it necessary to make his disclaimer. I think he was afraid that the allegorical dragon might gobble up the art and the myth.

Both Tolkien and Lewis have suggested that their stories began with images of people rather than with ideas. Tolkien says that hobbits first came from nowhere to him as he was reading student papers. The beginning was no moral or sociological or even religious idea, but an image. When I raised the question of motive, Professor Tolkien said simply, "I am a Christian and of course what I write will be from that essential viewpoint." Lewis was sure that "the only moral that is of any value is that which arises inevitably from the whole cast of the author's mind." Many of Tolkien's remarks on the story suggest that, behind the scene at least, there is a solid theistic world. He told Henry Resnik that the most moving point of the story for him is "when Gollum repents and tries to caress Frodo and he is interfered with by Sam." The tragedy is, he added, that "the good people so often upset the not-so-good people when they try to repent and it's a tragic moment."[7]

Secondly, one concerned with the possible Christian implications of the story will turn inevitably to Tolkien's famous essay on Faërie and particularly the last part of it in which he discusses the eucatastrophe and evangelium.

---

7. **Niekas**, No. 18, p. 39.

"The Birth of Christ," he says, "is the eucatastrophe of Man's history. The Resurrection is the eucatastrophe of the story of the Incarnation. . . . There is no tale ever told that men would rather find was true, and none which so many sceptical men have accepted as true on its own merits." It is as if one discovered a fairy-tale "primarily" true, that is, a real cinderella in your house or your neighborhood, or, better, the heavenly world made visible before your eyes. The joyful eucatastrophe of men's stories in its minor way echoes that of the greatest story of all, the descent of God to redeem men. The Evangelium in the story, even in the midst of a fallen world, gives "a fleeting glimpse of Joy, Joy beyond the walls of the world, poignant as grief."[8] Thus any story falling into the classification of Faërie, as defined by Tolkien, will be happily freighted with the highest "significatio" and redolent of heaven and eternal joy even if it never once mentions the name of Christ.

Thirdly, I think it not insignificant to take note of some remarks of Professor Tolkien in a publication of 1967 called **The Road Goes Ever On** which most Tolkien admirers are acquainted with. There he speaks, for the first time I believe, of Elbereth as "a 'divine' or 'angelic' person" and admits that elves and men and hobbits "invoke" her aid in time of trouble and that elves sing hymns to her, and then adds in parentheses the highly significant remark, "These and other references to religion in **The Lord of the Rings** are frequently overlooked." A little later he describes the Valar as presenting themselves to physical eyes clothed in "veils" or "raiment," being "self-incarnated" because of "their love and desire for the Children of God."[9] (This is, I think, the first time that the word "God" has ever been used by Tolkien in connection with **The Lord of the Rings**.) It is clear enough that the Valar may be quite properly

---

8. Tolkien, **Tree and Leaf**, p. 60.

9. **The Road Goes Ever On: A Song Cycle**; poems by J. R. R. Tolkien, music by Donald Swann (Boston: Houghton Mifflin, 1967), p. 66.

regarded as angels in the normal meaning of the term. When we have once acknowledged that fact, then it seems to me that the whole story must be given a strong spiritual or Biblical inference.

Thomas de Quincey pointed out that all great literature becomes "a Jacob's ladder from earth to mysterious altitudes above the earth" where a thoughtful reader may find meaning unlimited, and it is this sort of idea which gives credence to Guy Davenport's remark concerning Tolkien's story: "For a generation that can't make head or tail of St. Paul, Mr. Tolkien has got Isaiah and St. Paul back before readers' eyes." [10] He has indeed got the essence of St. Paul and Isaiah and the Biblical landscape before our eyes. Yet I for one will vote very strongly with Professor Tolkien against turning the story **simply** into Christian allegory. It is not allegory but myth. It is not a "statement" or a "system." It is a story to be enjoyed, not a sermon to be preached. Yet I think it is clear enough that for many readers the story deeply suggests the sadness of a paradise lost and the glory of one that can be regained.

---

10. Guy Davenport, "The Persistence of Light," **National Review**, April, 1965, p.334.

Unpublished Letter From
C. S. Lewis to Dr. Montgomery

This letter was written by Lewis in appreciation for Montgomery's article on the Narnian Chronicles which first appeared in print in 1959 and which constitutes Chapter V of the present volume. In his letter, Lewis gently expresses his humanist's impatience with the "age groups" of the social scientist. The copyright of this letter rests in the C. S. Lewis Estate.

21 Jan 1960

Dear Mr. Montgomery

Thank you for your kind

letter of the 14th and the enclosure. I need not say
that your article on the Narnian books gave me
much pleasure. I had thought of children rather
than adolescents as my readers, but have found
(wh. confirms your view) that they are read also
by schoolboys. But the truth is that my fan
mail makes hay of the (two popular) classificat-
-ion by Age Groups. It is types of people, at
whatever age, that really matter. By the bye, children
of 6 or 7, if brought up in Christian homes, usually
know who Aslan is quite as quickly as their elders.
Now for your questions. _Shadows of Ecstasy_ and
Essays presented to C. W. are both extremely hard to
get. But there are better 2d. hand booksellers than
Blackwell. I recommend Rogers, Bookseller, New-
-castle on Tyne (that is sufficient address). He
takes a great deal of trouble to find copies and

his changes are v. honest. As for other fiction of the "William-Lewis" brand, I don't know that any is now being produced — unless you include Tolkien's huge (and magnificent) 3 vol. romance The Lord of the Rings. Going back to the Victorians, you probably know already G. MacDonald's Lilith and Phantastes?

Under the Mercy
yours
C. S. Lewis

21 Jan 1960

Dear Mr. Montgomery

Thank you for your kind
letter of the 14th and the enclosure. I need not say
that your article on the Narnian books gave me
much pleasure. I had thought of children rather
than adolescents as my readers, but have found
(wh(ich) confirms your view) that they are read also
by schoolboys. But the truth is that my fan
mail makes hay of the (too popular) classificat-
-ion by Age-Groups. It is types of people, at
whatever age, that really matters. By the bye, children
of 6 or 7, if brought up in Christian homes, usually
know who Aslan is quite as quickly as their elders.
Now for your questions. **Shadows of Ecstasy**
[by Charles Williams] and **Essays presented to
C[harles] W[illiams]** are both extremely hard to
get.* But there are better 2d hand booksellers than
Blackwell. I recommend Rogers, Bookseller, New-
-castle on Tyne (that is sufficient address). He
takes a great deal of trouble to find copies and
his charges are v[ery] honest. As for other fiction of
the "Williams-Lewis" hand, I don't know that
any is now being produced—unless you can
include Tolkien's huge (and magnificent) 3
vol. romance **The Lord of the Rings**. Going
back to the Victorians, you probably know
already G. MacDonald's **Lilith** and **Phantastes**?

Under the Mercy
yours
C. S. Lewis

*[In 1960—**Editor**.]

Revue Critique*

Clyde S. Kilby, *The Christian World of C. S. Lewis*. Appleford,
Abington, Berks., Marcham Manor Press, 1965. 216 p.

Qui était Clive Staples Lewis? Dans le monde anglophone
cette question serait superflue puisqu'avant sa mort, en 1963,
sa réputation était solidement établie dans le domaine de
la connaissance littéraire comme dans celui de la littérature
religieuse. Mais dan les pays d'expression francaise on le con-
naît à peine, et c'est dommage, car c'est un des ècrivains
littéraires et théologiques les plus importants du vingtième
siècle. Le critique littéraire David Daiches a dit avec raison
que, de son vivant, les écrits apologétiques de Lewis en faveur
de la foi chrétienne ont contribué, plus que n'importe quelle
autre influence, à produire un réveil religieux in Angleterre.

Fort à propos, le meilleur ouvrage sur la vie et la pensée
de Lewis a été écrit par un autre érudit littéraire. Lewis
termina sa carrière comme professeur de littérature du Moyen
Age et de la Renaissance à l'Université de Cambridge; son
biographe, qui le connaissait personnellement, est professeur
d'anglais dans une institution chrétienne distinguée : Wheaton
College (près de Chicago). Leurs intérêts communs ont permis

---

* *Revue d'Histoire et de Philosophie Religieuses*, LI/2 (1971), 213-14.

à Kilby d'écrire une biographie unique qui devrait être lue par tous ceux qui veulent comprendre, la carrière, les oeuvres et l'influence de Lewis. Ce livre est bien supérieur à d'autres ouvrages sure le même sujet, par exemple celui de Richard B. Cunningham : C. S. LEWIS : DEFENDER OF THE FAITH (Westminster, 1967). Les seuls livres qui l'on peut comparer favorablement à celui de Kilby sont : C. S. LEWIS : APOSTLE TO THE SKEPTICS (MacMillan, 1949) de Chad Walsh, et C. S. LEWIS (Henry Walck, 1963), de Roger Lancelyn Green—mais ces deux ouvrages sont difficiles à obtenir et ils sont moins étendus que l'ouvrage de Kilby.

Lewis était, avant tout, un apologiste; d'après l'opinion du critique qui écrit ces lignes, il a été le meilleur apologiste du christianisme historique à paraître dans notre siècle. En tant qu'athée converti au christianisme à l'âge adulte, Lewis se rendait compte avec acuité qu'un grand nombre d'intellectuals incroyants n'avaient jamais été mis en face du message chrétien authentique, et moins encore en face des faits nombreux qui prouvent sa véracité. Il s'est donc donné comme tâche de faire connaître aux non-chrétiens l'essentiel de la foi chrétienne—dans le langage de nos jours, sans utiliser le vocabulaire technique des théologiens professionnels—et il a essayé, en même temps, de les confronter avec le grand éventail de preuves qui étayent la véracité de la foi. L'un des aspects les plus saisissants de la technique apologétique de Lewis est son refus d'atténuer le contenu de la foi chrétienne pour le faire accepter plus facilement par les incrédules contemporains. En contraste frappant avec John A. T. Robinson (*Dieu Sans Dieu*), il soutient la solidité historique et philosophique des récits bibliques de miracles, la réalité de la chute et de la rédemption de l'homme et la véracité de fait de la doctrine de la Trinité, selon la formule de Nicée. Lewis croyait que ces vérités chrétiennes pouvaient être défendues contre l'incrédulité et que la même sorte de raisonnement que le non-chrétien utilise dans sa vie quotidienne, s'il est appliqué conséquemment, le confronte nécessairement avec les affirmations de Jésus-Christ. Il ne peut plus, dès lors, rejeter Jésus-Christ à cause des preuves contre l'évangile, mais il le fait en dépit de toutes les preuves qui soutiennent la validité de la foi.

Ici, sur le continent, où l'influence de Bultmann a changé l'orientation théologique de la considération sérieuse des

affirmations cognitives du Nouveau Testament à leur réinter-
prétation existentielle et où l'approche de Dieu par Barth
comme L'Entièrement Autre (dans les termes de Rudolph
Otto) tend à dévaluer tous les efforts apologétiques aux yeux
des incroyants, l'oeuvre de C. S. Lewis mérite la plus sérieuse
considération.

Les lecteurs français qui souhaiteraient entrer en contact
avec Lewis dans leur propre langue, peuvent se procurer les
ouvrages suivants : SURPRIS PAR LA JOIE (Editions du Seuil)
—une autobiographie spirituelle de Lewis; LE PROBLEME DE
LA SOUFFRANCE (Desclée de Brouwer)—sur le problème
classique du mal; et les quatre livres suivants qui montrent
comment Lewis a utilisé l'allégorie littéraire, le mythe et le
roman de fiction pour communiquer le message chrétien : TAC-
TIQUE DU DIABLE (Delachaux et Niestlé), LE GRAND
DIVORCE ENTRE LE CIEL ET LA TERRE (Delachaux et
Niestlé), LE SILENCE DE LA TERRE (Gallimard), et LE
LION ET LA SORCIERE BLANCHE (Hachette). Quant aux
Allemands, nous leurs recommandons de lire avec beaucoup
d'attention DIE LETZTE NACHT DER WELT : GEISTLICHE
ESSAYS (Hamburg: Furche-Verlag), comme exemple de l'hab-
ileté de Lewis en tant qu'essayiste apologétique. Après ce
contact avec les oeuvres de Lewis, la lecture du livre de Kilby
sera la moyen idéal de voir tous les aspects du génie de Lewis
dans une perspective plus large.

John Warwick Montgomery

The Contributors

EDMUND FULLER is a writer, critic, and teacher. His books include four novels, **A Star Pointed North, Brothers Divided, The Corridor**, and **Flight**, and such diversified non-fiction as **Man in Modern Fiction, John Milton, Successful Calamity**, and **Affirmations of God and Man**. His reviews and articles have appeared in **The New York Times, Saturday Review, The American Scholar**, and other media. He has taught at Columbia University, Kent School, and St. Stephen's School, Rome. While at Kent, he edited a symposium volume, **The Christian Idea of Education**, bringing together the contributions of Alan Paton, Reinhold Niebuhr, Jacques Maritain, Georges Florovsky, William Pollard, Harris Harbison, and other distinguished Christian thinkers. Mr. Fuller's concern with the writers treated in the present volume is evident from his **Books with Men behind Them**, about half of which is devoted to essays on Lewis, Tolkien, and Williams, and from his **Introduction and Commentary to Charles Williams' "All Hallows' Eve"**, in Seabury's "Religious Dimensions in Literature" series.

CLYDE S. KILBY (Ph.D., New York University) has recently retired from a long and memorable career as Professor and Chairman of the English Department at Wheaton College (Illinois). Though a writer of scholarly works in the general field of literature (**Poetry and Life, Christianity and Aesthetics**), he is best known for his special interest in C. S. Lewis and his circle. Dr. Kilby's book, **The Christian World of C. S. Lewis,** has rapidly attained the status of a classic (see Professor Montgomery's French review of it in the Appendix to the present volume). He has produced **A Mind Awake,** anthologizing Lewis' sayings and ideas, and has edited a book of Lewis' letters under the title, **Letters to an American Lady.** His personal recollections of Lewis have recently been included in Carolyn Keefe's **C. S. Lewis: Speaker & Teacher.** An essay on Williams from his pen appeared in the March, 1971, issue of **HIS Magazine.** Dr. Kilby spent the summer of 1966 in Oxford, helping Tolkien with his new epic, **The Silmarillion,** and the fruit of that association can be seen in his several published articles on the author of **The Lord of the Rings** (inter alia: "The Lost Myth," in the Summer-Fall, 1969, issue of **Arts in Society,** and "Meaning in **The Lord of the Rings,**" in **Shadows of Imagination,** edited by Mark Hillegas). In 1971, Professor Kilby was honored by a Festschrift (**Imagination and the Spirit,** edited by Charles A. Huttar), in which an entire section is devoted to essays on Lewis, Williams, Tolkien, and their spiritual and literary forerunner, George MacDonald; Chad Walsh wrote the entertaining Foreword.

RUSSELL KIRK (Litt. D., St. Andrews, Scotland), is best known for the book he wrote to fulfill his doctoral dissertation requirement: **The Conservative Mind,** which established him as the leading philosopher of the new American political conservatism. He has taught at Michigan State, University of Detroit, Long Island University, and the New School for Social Research, but now devotes his energies to a full schedule of lecturing and to prolific writing. His books range from political theory (**A Program for Conservatives**) to novels (**Old House of Fear**), from educational philosophy (**Academic Freedom**) and social criticism (**Beyond the Dreams of Avarice**) to ghost stories (**The Surly Sullen Bell**). (Dr. Montgomery, as author of a book on the occult, particularly appreciated Dr. Kirk's account, while a dinner guest of the Montgomerys, of a true spectral happening at his ancestral home in Mecosta, Michigan!) Dr. Kirk's empathy with Chesterton is understandable in light of our essayist's conversion from the ranks of the unchurched to Roman Catholicism in 1964.

JOHN WARWICK MONTGOMERY (Ph.D., Chicago; D. Théol., Strasbourg, France) is professor-elect of Law and Theology at the International School of Law, Washington, D.C. Before assuming this position, he served for ten years as Professor and Chairman of the Division of Church History and History of Christian Thought at Trinity Evangelical Divinity School, Deerfield, Illinois; while at Trinity, he spent half of each year directing the seminary's European Graduate Theological Studies Program at the University of Strasbourg, France, and continues to reside in Strasbourg during the summers. On alternate years at the University of Strasbourg he taught a course on "The Literary and Theological Apologetic of C. S. Lewis." He also functions as the Executive Director of European Operations for the Christian Research Institute in Strasbourg. He is author of twenty-five books (English, French, German, Spanish) in theology, philosophy, history, and related fields, and serves as editor of the **International Scholars Directory** and Lippincott's "Evangelical Perspectives" series. In recent years Dr. Montgomery has come to be known as the foremost American theological spokeman for "confessional" Protestantism; in 1968, he was chosen to represent this position, over against fundamentalism, liberalism, and the death-of-God viewpoint, in **Spectrum of Protestant Beliefs**, edited by Robert Campbell, O.P. He has been in public dialog-debate with the late Bishop James Pike, Thomas J. J. Altizer, and Joseph Fletcher. His "Ninety-Five These for the 450th Anniversary of the Reformation" created a considerable stir in Germany, where they were published alongside Luther's in 1967. Dr. Montgomery's interest in the writers discussed in the present volume began with his conversion to Christianity in 1948, in part owing to the influence on him of C. S. Lewis' publications. Subsequently he corresponded with Lewis, who wrote of Montgomery's **History & Christianity**: "I don't think it could be bettered."

CHAD WALSH (Ph.D., Michigan) is Professor and Chairman of the Department of English and Writer-in-Residence at Beloit College. He is an adult convert from agnosticism to Christianity, and was much influenced in his spiritual pilgrimage by the writings of T. S. Eliot. His concern with the work of Lewis was first reflected in his book, **C. S. Lewis: Apostle to the Skeptics**, still the finest treatment of Lewis as apologist. Subsequently, he dealt with Lewis' "Impact on America" in **Light on C. S. Lewis**, by a roster of distinguished contributors, headed by Owen Barfield. In Hillegas' **Shadows of Imagination**, Professor Walsh provided the opening essay: "C. S. Lewis: The Man and the Mystery." Among more than a dozen books on other subjects, Dr. Walsh has written **Campus Gods on Trial, Early Christians of the 21st Century, From Utopia to Nightmare,** and **God at Large,** and five volumes of his own verse, including **The End of Nature**. He is much in demand on American campuses for readings of his poetry, and has served as a Fulbright Lecturer in Rome and Finland. In 1964 he was the first Protestant to receive the annual Spirit Award of the Catholic Poetry Society of America.

Index